CAMP
HERO

A Story of
Spiritual Healing

CHARLES F. CARLINO

Library of Congress Cataloging-in-Publication Data
ISBN: 1466283092
ISBN-13: 978-1466283091

To contact the author, visit:
www.CampHero-FriendsOnTheWall.com

GIFT IN A PERFECT WORLD

In a perfect world
we can bare our souls

In return the Universe
offers the gift of love

This story is
my gift to you

I wish you a Universe
of love and happiness

GOD BLESS

DEDICATION

My deepest appreciation to my lovely wife Anna,
You have taught me to see with my heart and open my
Soul to Dance with the Universe.
I have been blessed, for you are my Angel from
The heavens "444"
You are a true and kind person,
my spiritual teacher and a wonderful wife.
Thank you for helping me to reconstruct the rubble
and bring this story to a special place.
To my dear friend and hero, Joseph Giannini
Your life has inspired me.
You are truly a man above men and a surf brother.
To all who share the Brotherhood of Life
the Firemen, Policemen, Families and Victims
alive and departed, all who were part of the tragedy of
September 11, 2001.
To my Brothers and Sisters of the Armed Forces,
you all wear the Medal of Honor.
My thanks and gratitude to those heroes
on the frontlines at home and far away,
We will never understand what it takes to fill your shoes.
We are the Land of the Free,
Because of the Brave!
God Bless You All.

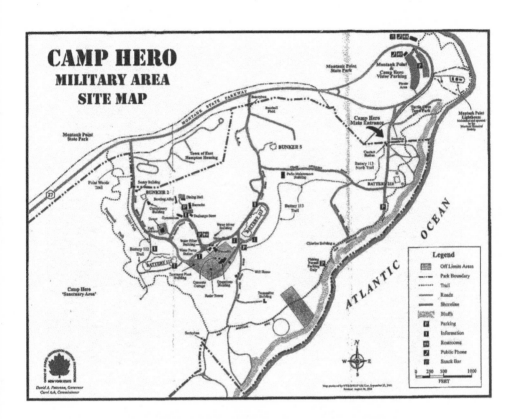

CAMP HERO STATE PARK
MONTAUK, LONG ISLAND, NY

INTRODUCTION

Our story unfolds…it's the year 2001, a time of peace and prosperity. The world is a friendly place. The vision of optimism fills the streets and towns across our nation. A seasoned workforce is about to retire and live out the American Dream. A new generation is entering the workplace, eager to fill the shoes of their predecessors. The perception of a mighty nation and a mighty people—invisible to the threat of a foreign enemy—was just that…a perception. The thought of war seemed like an old, dusty novel sitting on a bookshelf. Then, one beautiful September morning, our country was attacked and our world thrown into chaos. 9/11 had arrived.

Two damaged souls, from two different worlds, Vietnam Veteran, US Marine Corp. Captain, Joseph A. Gianinni, Esq., and Annette Mary O'Gorman, survivor of 9/11, are about to meet and share their black box of life, taking a spiritual journey to find a place of healing.

* * *

On the shores of Eastern Long Island, at the place known as "The End," stands a mighty lighthouse, casting its majestic beam for more than a century bridging the time between two worlds.

High on the steep, rocky bluffs flanking its western border, you can still see the remains of a fortress, the skeleton of a once thriving outpost still active with the many souls who lived and died there serving our great nation during World War II. It is here among the ruins that our story comes alive, offering an answer to the pain and suffering from the tragic loss of loved ones.

It is here at Camp Hero we begin to heal.

THE STORY

EMPIRE STATE

A beam of light races through the galaxy…maybe a quasar, supernova or the birth of a star.

A planet evolves for billions of years, waiting for this world to arrive and for a brief moment this stage of life to play out.

Gases spin, creating microorganisms and primordial forms of life. Dinosaurs roaming the earth for millions of years— in a flash—become extinct. The first signs of man are found suspended in ice as if frozen there only days ago.

Sailors from the Far East, braving thousands of miles in treacherous seas to reach the shores of this New Continent, commence the creation of new civilizations: the Aztecs, Incas and Mayans introduce the first intelligent life to this new world, witnessing these ancestral tribes feeding this tree of life, bringing us to modern day man.

They all share one common link embedded in their DNA, a gene that ties together all life to one place in time. Millions of years bring us to a single moment on this magical planet, where every living species is known to have been derived.

A view from outer space has identified this "hot spot" beaming as the brightest star in our galaxy, sending its pulsar out to the heavens, awaiting an answer.

Man was placed here for good reason. In this vast universe, galaxies sail through dark matter in the veins of God's lifeblood.

1

Our world is part of this lifeblood, making us one with God. From infinitesimal particles, tinier than atoms, to the immense boundless reaches of the universe, we are all part of this dream called life—and as cells who live and die, our existence is part of the grand scheme.

There in the distance lies a newfound promised land. For the first time ever, representatives of these ancient tribes can sit around and share a voice.

For the first time ever, God's messengers could set up shop side by side and share their beliefs.

For the first time in history, men and women from every race, creed and color can experience the freedom to choose their path toward reaching their goals and aspirations.

This unique organism, with its veracious appetite for the human race, shines as a beacon to life.

This one place—

This one Mecca—

This one shrine—

New York City.

The sun rises on a bright, new day as a young woman makes her way down the steps of a brownstone toward the street and hails a taxi.

From the backseat, dressed in a black dress and high heels, she gazes out the window as the taxi inches its way in the early morning rush-hour traffic across the Manhattan Bridge. She stares at the BMT subway and the many faces of straphangers making their way to work just as they have been for over a century.

Reaching the summit of the bridge, the unidentified woman peers through the opposite window framing the World Trade Towers, creating a monolithic reflection in the new day sun.

Today, the world lies solid beneath her feet. With a pocket full of dreams for an aspiring future, she is determined to take all the gifts that this tree of life has to offer.

It hasn't been easy. The dues have been paid, sacrifices made; with challenges to overcome, she stands ready to take her rightful place in society. The taxi makes its way down Broadway, the street bustling with the energy of a fine-tuned workforce unlike any other in the world. Reaching their destination, the taxi pulls to the curb as the woman boldly steps out onto the street slamming the door behind her.

She has arrived.

DAWN PATROL

A clock buzzes 4 a.m. on a cold, dark winter morning. A man awakens from his warm, deep sleep, reaching over his wife to turn off the alarm. Sitting up on the side of the bed, he runs his fingers through his hair, rises and stumbles into the bathroom. His wife turns over and curls up into a fetal position, remaining asleep.

Turning on the bathroom light, he stares into the mirror to see the reflection of a rough, unshaven face. Reaching for a toothbrush, he squeezes out some toothpaste; lifting the toilet seat, he stands and with a long yawn relieves himself. Quietly he heads downstairs to the kitchen. Here at the end of Long Island, in this popular modern-day beach community, a small group of men—blue collar workers, husbands, fathers, professionals—all share one tradition: they are hardcore surfers. Out here they take their surfing and their brotherhood serious, a ritual that has been created and followed to a spiritual level.

To these men, surfing is not about life or death—it's more important than that. Each day they perform their worldly duties as mild-mannered members of society and then in an instant, the brotherhood calls, stripping their social identity, revealing their essence. For in life, they are first and foremost surfers.

Joseph Giannini, prominent criminal defense attorney and decorated Vietnam Veteran of the United States Marine Corps, pours a glass of orange juice, grabs a duffel bag and

5

wetsuit, steps outside into the cold morning air. Jumping into his classic 1979 Jeep Wagoneer, with surfboard mounted on the roof, he turns the key to the ignition and after a few attempts, his surf relic finally starts. Vapor from his breath fogs the windshield as he heads out on this early morning mission mustering his troops in preparation for the battle that lies ahead.

The truck bounces to the intersection at Hog Creek Road; he makes a left. Driving a short distance, he arrives at a small, white cottage set back in a line of pine trees. The glow of a cigarette pierces the morning darkness. Mike, a local fireman, appears from the driveway. Hoisting up his surfboard, he secures it onto the roof rack and jumps into the passenger seat. The two roll on to their next stop. Few words are shared between them as Mike turns on the static-ridden radio to search for a weather report. With no success, they settle for a station playing '60s rock.

Joe pulls into a long, winding driveway that leads them to a large, modern home recently built by a Wall Street businessman. A honk of the horn summons a middle-aged man from the house with his gear hung over his shoulder. He mounts his surfboard, then jumps into the backseat. Charles, a sixty-year-old Veteran Marine, breaks the morning silence. "What the hell are we doing? It's 4:30 in the morning. This is crazy, it's freezing!"

After a quick laugh, the silence resumes. The group pushes on, picking up Alex and Vick along the way.

The men head east along a twelve-mile stretch of highway

searching out a number of surf breaks. Mike finally locates the 5 a.m. surf report that is barely audible through the static.

This is the 5 a.m. surf advisory. Hard winds coming out of the north at 15 to 20 mph, water temperature 36 degrees, air temperature 34 degrees, high tide at 11:45 a.m., sunrise 6:35 a.m., wave height 6 to 10 feet and building, early-morning conditions single to double overhead and clean. Get on it early. Winds will shift to the southeast by afternoon.

Suddenly the group comes alive as Vick yells, "The ditch will be perfect!"

Charles refutes, "The ditch is a bitch, we can do her anytime. Let's do Turtles."

Repeatedly honking the horn, Joe shouts, "We're going to the Camp!"

The men respond in unison, "Let's do it!"

Silence returns, the troops push on.

A worn sign marks the sleepy town of Montauk, two miles ahead. In the distance, a cluster of light beams appears out of the darkness. As they approach, a number of vehicles become visible. Joe pulls in, met by a group of surfers tightly huddled together in the frigid morning air. All the members of this fraternity embrace in a familiar ritual: the coffee shop is their last link with civilization before going forward into the abyss.

The men grab their coffee, sharing a few last words with their comrades in preparation for their final assault on the lighthouse. Returning to the car, the level of excitement is high as they speed off in anticipation of the great surf that lies ahead. Passing a sign, Montauk Point 6 miles ahead, the caravan rolls on.

Upon arriving at their destination, the ghostly silhouette of the Montauk lighthouse comes into view. Suddenly Joe slows down. Looking to his right, he spots a sign next to a dirt trail announcing Camp Hero. Turning hard, they descend the bumpy gravel road. An eerie feeling pierces their mood as they pass through an abandoned ghost of a checkpoint, resembling a small telephone booth with its wooden gate locked in the upright position. Navigating the deeply rutted trail, they reach an open field at the edge of the bluff, where a parking area has been carved out of tall sea grass by the fishermen and surfers who frequent this area.

Surfers are not particularly welcome here, as the fishermen have always competed for the rights to use this habitat. Joe parks the car; the men scramble to the end of the hundred-foot bluff to view the ocean and the surf break on the beach below. All are locked in on the swell that lies before them, as if God laid out a beautiful silk carpet to their destiny. Excitement fills the frigid air, the surf is huge, and the men are stoked.

Going into action, they un-strap their surfboards from the rack and set them onto the lumpy grass pods that make up the top of the bluff. Duffel bags in hand, they move to the end of the parking lot to a small brick building marked public restrooms. They begin to change into their combat gear. The distinct hiss of a single-steam radiator is heard in between the commotion of rumbling bags and gear. Stripped bare, they methodically apply the protective layers that will insulate them from the icy waters. Booties, gloves and head cap complete their armament.

With zippers drawn, the platoon files out. Taking their boards, they work their way down the steep path to the beach. An eerie feeling lingers as they pass the silhouettes of the many haunted remains of bunkers and pillboxes that once protected our great nation during the last war. They move in stealth-like silence.

Marching through the thick canopy that covers the trail to the sea, they eagerly approach the beach. The roar of surf is announced by the clamoring of boulders colliding in the shore break. This distinct sound engages their already heightened senses.

Finally the troops arrive onto the beach to a magnificent, surreal vision. The stars are still visible in the magical pre-dawn sky. The moonlit trail evokes the presence of God, as if He were there just moments ago, putting the finishing touches on his masterpiece for his sons to discover.

With the sign of the cross, Captain Giannini leads his men through the darkness as they paddle out with caution to avoid every surfer's nightmare—getting caught on the inside, where the white water rules. The band intensely follows between the ebbs and flows of this incoming fire. Paddling to the outside, Joe takes the point position, his men deployed, locked, cocked and ready for action.

Off this rocky shore where the water swells and the waves form like heavily fortified infantry lines coming to do battle, the men look to Joe for his leadership once again. A man above men, a respected leader in the lineup, Mr. Giannini, free and confident, projects his wartime horror to create this surreal battlefield. Having stood by his side through many battles, they look to him as their supreme leader...for here Mr. Giannini lives and...here Mr. Giannini reigns.

Taking up the flank position, they prepare for their assault as the first set of waves heaves forward. Alex goes right dropping out of view with the water in steamy pursuit. All eyes follow. The wave attacks the rocks as Alex appears gloriously catapulted into the air. With a hearty scream, he announces his conquest.

Standing ready and confident in their leader, working as a fine-tuned unit, each takes his position, peeling off wave after wave. Attacking the beachhead, nervous but fearless to the mission at hand, they will conquer.

Dave attempts to take off late on a fast-forming left and disappears over the falls in a horrendous closeout. All look on attentively. When Dave finally surfaces, the men signal all is well.

The first set passes just as the sun peeks over the horizon, announcing the dawn of man. A primeval feeling grips the band of heroes doing battle while the world sleeps.

Joe, perched in the ready for the big push, watches proudly as his men repel wave after wave. Then followed by a lull, peace returns and all wonder, "Has this dream come to an end?" Suddenly the sea begins to rear its head; they know what lies before them. Scrambling to find the safety of the outside position, they realize the heavy artillery of the cleanup set is bearing down on them. With bayonets drawn, they prepare to engage in hand-to-hand combat.

All look to their leader as he single handedly takes on the first wave, an attack of epic proportion. Confident, Joe rises to do battle with a power and fury greater than all the armies of all times. Slashing down the side of this beast, he carves the first blow. Ripping through its curled back, the monster begins to bleed as foam spews from its side. Again it rears its head enraged, engulfing Joe in its arms as to squeeze the life from its victim. Strangled deep within its grasp, Joe strikes a blow with a vicious cutback, repeating this over and over till he severs the dragon's head. The beast finally lying at his feet, victorious Joe turns to the sea and rejoins his troops.

Waves of reinforcements now line the beach as far as the eye could see. Secure in his imaginary world, he has fought the perfect war, a war without casualty. Turning screams of horror to screams of joy, surfing is his salvation. He orders his men to stand-down.

"Sir, the beachhead is secure."

**CAPTAIN JOSEPH GIANNINI
DECORATED VIETNAM VETERAN
UNITED STATES MARINE CORPS**

FRIENDLY FIRE

The typical Sunday night drive from East Hampton is a single-lane highway jammed with weekend warriors heading home to make the Monday morning bell. This Monday is particularly important for Joe, who is due in court at 10 a.m. to sum up for the defense in the most difficult case of his career. A Panamanian ex con has been indicted for Murder One, the shooting of an undercover New York City police officer and the attempted murder of the officer's partner.

Making a pit stop, Vicky, Joe's wife of twenty-one years, steps out of their 1987 Mercedes Benz and returns with two cups of coffee, passing them through the window for the ride home. In healthy masculine style, Joe gives his beautiful, bright, voluptuous blond wife the once-over as she leans through the window exposing her deep cleavage in a low-cut sweater. Preoccupied by the ride home and the case that follows, he regrets not sharing an intimate moment before they departed.

Picking up on Joe's body language, Vicky blushes like a teenage girl, warning him to keep his eyes on the road. Joe smiles, wondering how many years will it take man to successfully gape at a woman without getting caught. The two spend the rest of the ride pleasantly aroused, with Joe fantasizing about the car breaking down on some deserted road, leaving him and Vicky stranded.

Three hours later, they arrive at their brownstone on the

upper west side of Manhattan. After unloading the car, Joe searches the neighborhood for a parking space while Vicky settles in for the evening changing into a blue lace nighty. Entering the apartment, he makes a beeline for the bedroom, where the two engage in a moment of heated passion.

They awake as the phone rings over to a message. The voice on the other end is his client, Rinaldo Rayside, voicing a last plea for freedom. Joe rolls out of Vicky's arms and heads downstairs to the dining room, which for the last three months has been converted into a war room in his quest to uncover his client's innocence.

In the year leading up to the trial, the shootings have been on the media's front burner. The coverage has been intensely prejudicial to his client and their line of defense, going so far as to mock him on the nightly news. It's August 1999, a month into the trial. The prosecution is claiming that Joe's client attacked an officer working anti-crime and that during the ensuing struggle he disarmed and killed the officer with his own revolver. The surviving partner has already testified to the above. He has also testified that during a wild shootout, Rayside tried to kill him, too. However, all the forensic evidence—autopsy, ballistics, and crime-scene investigation—indicates that the officer was killed by a distant shot, a shot that deflected off a hard object, possibly a car bumper, and into the officer's back.

Most damning to the prosecution, Joe's private investigator has found an eyewitness who contradicts the surviving partner's version. The defense witness has testified that she heard a shot, went to a window and saw a white male fire more shots toward several men who were in a scuffle up the block. Her sworn testimony indicated that the shooter could be the surviving partner or another police officer.

Before the trial began, Joe visited the District Attorney's office many times to examine evidence and procure additional discovery. On several occasions, he ran into the surviving police officer, who each time bowed his head and looked away from Joe. A strange reaction. He had seen it before, but where? When?

The huge case file—testimony transcripts, discovery documents and copies of exhibits—is spread across the Giannini's dining room table. Joe has read it all and cannot find a way to shape it into a story to tell the jury. He believes based on the evidence and lack thereof, the police are covering up a scandal: the accidental killing of an off-duty police officer by his off-duty partner or another, unknown off-duty officer during a shakedown. Suddenly he recalls an incident from many years ago. A killing, a cover-up, it's coming back to him. The past is reaching up to the present, revealing the truth. He couldn't see it because he was blinded by his own guilt. He knows now he must go back.

At 10 a.m., Joe stands and begins his summation. Approximately two hours later, he takes the jury back In Country to August 1967.

Every Marine sent to Nam had to do a thirteen-month tour. Each had a rotation date, the day he would leave the field for home. Dead Marines in most situations were wrapped in their own ponchos and quickly choppered away. We called this poncho rotation. This practice left their friends without a chance to properly mourn them. We suspect that this quick removal of the dead Marines was calculated: out of sight, out of mind…

* * *

Joe takes the jury back...

He arrived In Country early July 1967 and joined the First Battalion, Third Marines, a.k.a., "The Home of The Brave." Joe took command of the 81mm-mortar platoon. Their platoon leader had just been killed in the DMZ, short for the Dead Marine Zone.

A week later he was reassigned to a rifle platoon, Bravo One, B Company. When he picked up Bravo One, he had the good luck of getting an outstanding platoon sergeant. He knew as soon as he met Staff Sergeant Head that this man was a survivor. Better stick close. Up to mid-August, his platoon had suffered only four Wounded in Action (WIAs), three were injured by booby-traps and one from friendly artillery.

The sun was starting to cast shadows as Bravo Company moved onto a small hill next to a deserted village, as high ground has distinct military advantages. Joe receives a radio call from the company commander, Captain Landes.

"Bravo One, this is Bravo Six, over."

"Bravo Six, this is Bravo One, over."

"Bravo One, come on up, out."

Joe joined the company commander and the two other platoon leaders. Captain Landes said, "We're setting in, three-man holes. He wants each platoon to send out a four-man listening post. Code name: Snoopy. Follow me, I'll show you your platoon sectors." The men then trailed off at a quick pace.

Upon returning to his platoon, Joe called Staff Sergeant Head, the Platoon Sergeant, Sergeant Falafeni, the Platoon Guide, and his two squad leaders. "We're setting in. Sergeant King your squad has a listening post. Four men, Code name: Snoopy One. OK, follow me." As they moved, he indicated where to put each fighting hole and each of the two machine-gun teams. They dug in, ate C-rations and divided their night watches. Just as the sun was about to disappear behind the distant mountains to their west, Bravo Six radioed down: "Stand to."

He relayed the order to Bravo One. Every Marine stopped whatever he was doing, got into his fighting hole and faced outboard. This important ritual was performed every dusk and dawn. The orders "Lights out" meant: No smoking. No fires. No unnecessary noise. Out there, any kind of light can be seen from a great distance. Even whispers travel very far. The point men were sent out one hundred meters into the deserted village.

That evening, Joe had gotten the 1 a.m. to 3 a.m. watch. During each watch, he walked the lines several times, making sure at least one Marine was awake and alert in each fighting hole. That night on his first round, when he approached the first machine gun team position, someone whispered, "Be careful, Lieutenant. It's steep and slippery here." He recognized the voice as Machine Gunner Joseph Listorti.

He remembered the first time they met. He had just taken over the platoon and made his first amphibious landing with them. They advanced over a wide beach to a long line of towering sand dunes. They stayed in the dunes and dug in as night approached. Sometime during that dark night, he walked the lines, for his first time, with Platoon Sergeant Head. During the walk, they'd stopped at the first machine gun position and a Marine said to Head, "How's the new Lieutenant?"

Head replied, "I don't know, why don't you ask him yourself?"

Then from the same Marine, "Oh shit, I mean sorry, Sir!"

Head turned to Joe and said, "Sir, this is machine gunner Joseph Listorti."

Joe walked by, checking the remaining positions, and returned to his own. It was 2 a.m. on this unusually quiet, cloudy night when he decided to check with the point men again.

"Snoopy One, this is Bravo One. If clear click twice, if not click once."

One click.

He reached over and shook Staff Sergeant Head awake. "We have movement."

Next, he got Sergeant Falafeni and they ran off to make sure everyone was on alert. He surveyed the lines. Marines in their fighting positions, Joe noticed the machine gunner to his right had moved forward to get a better field of fire.

The platoon knew to hold its fire.

Suddenly, a racket of small-arms fire arose from the village. The point men had made contact. Everyone crouched lower as rounds started whizzing into their lines. Without permission, Snoopy One was moving back.

Joe shouted, "Hold your fire, the point men are coming in!" The firing ceased.

But he heard "Corpsman, Corpsman" coming from the machine gun team to his right. He ran over. Staff Sergeant Head was already there. Snoopy One was coming through their lines. He bent down and kneeled alongside the downed gunner, blood oozing from his left eye. He heard his soft moaning.

"He's dying," Sergeant Head said. "Lieutenant, look at his helmet." Pointing to a small hole in front, he said, "This wasn't an AK-47 round, this is a small-caliber round, an M-16." The soldier's moaning was barely audible.

Joe looked around for Snoopy One. The men were standing nearby. He approached and asked, "Did you get any incoming?" Bowed heads, no eye contact, no response. In that instant, he realized their fear had made them panic, and their panic caused them to run, firing wildly into their own lines.

Staff Sergeant Head called him back to where the machine gunner had fallen and confirmed, "He's dead. Do you know who it is?"

"Joseph Listorti."

Sergeant Head then said, "Lieutenant, Joseph has already finished his tour and was rotating home on the next chopper."

"I didn't know."

As they wrapped Joseph in his poncho, they heard the Medevac chopper coming for him.

The night was quiet now. Joseph Listorti was on his way home. Joe thought about Joseph's mother and father waiting for him. His suffering was over, but theirs was about to begin. It would be unbearable and unending.

They'll report his death as killed in action by enemy fire.

Under Joe's command, the platoon had suffered its first killed in action. It was a bad omen Joseph Listorti had completed his tour, killed by another Marine.

With his head down in regret, Joe confesses...

"I'd have gone crazy if I kept thinking about this. I wouldn't have been able to function. I'd have gotten killed, or worse, caused other Marines to get killed. I blocked this out. I pushed Joseph's death and my guilt down into a dark space and kept them there. Suddenly my left shoulder began to twitch, stopping about a minute later. Then my right eyelid started. It didn't stop twitching until I was on a plane back to the world. Today, I live a life sentence of knowing that Joseph's father and mother went to their graves not knowing the truth about their son's death. His three sisters still believe he was killed by enemy fire. I never told anyone that a fellow Marine killed him. I covered it up, and that is just what happened here."

He turns from the jury and faces the spectators.

Raising his right arm, Joe points to the surviving police officer and says, "There's the guilt."

* * *

Two days later, Joe arrives in court. His client Rinaldo Rayside is acquitted. In a flash, the fate of an innocent man is saved by the justice system.

Embracing his client, they leave the courthouse faced with the clamor of photographers and the press with reporters still posing pointed questions of suspicion at an innocent man.

Joe, avoiding interviews, jumps in a taxi and heads to the airport to catch a 4 p.m. flight for California to take part in the Vietnam Veterans Surf Memorial Paddle-Out.

With thoughts of the tens of thousands of men and women who served and died in the Vietnam War, he wonders:

"Where is their justice? Where is their pardon?"

He boards the plane.

ENCHANTED EVENING

A buzzer rings announcing the end of the school day at P.S. 77, an elementary school in Park Slope Brooklyn. A teacher helps her children tidy up before their trip home. The third-grade class lines up in the hallway and begins filing out of the building.

Passing by the administration office, Annette punches out and submits the usual paperwork for a substitute teacher working in the Brooklyn school system. Tossing her bag over her shoulder, she joins a colleague and heads for the subway, taking her favorite route up Third Street through the rich turn-of-the-century neighborhood where the grandest of brownstones resides. Arriving at Parkside, they walk ten blocks to Grand Army Plaza where they say their goodbyes.

Checking her phone before descending to the subway, Annette retrieves her messages: "Hi Annette, this is Brenda. Miss you, let's get together."

She forwards to the second message, charmed by a soft, deep handsome voice: "Hello, I'm looking for a beautiful young woman to join me at 7 p.m. for champagne and dinner at the Plaza. If you accept, please press one."

Annette stands frozen amidst the armies of people converging on the elaborately carved Arc de Triomphe of Brooklyn, laughing at her husband Dan's invitation to join him for a mystical evening of romance and intrigue. While dating in college, Dan would whisk Annette away in his imaginary time machine on a magical journey of Manhattan during the turn of the century. All of this on a shoestring budget, fifteen dollars to be exact.

* * *

At 7 p.m. sharp, Annette descends the steps to the lower level of the Plaza Hotel for a rendezvous at Charlie's Clam Bar. Dressed in a seductive white lace Victorian gown she inherited from her grandmother, she meets her date.

Daniel stands at the bar, a tall, handsome black-haired, blue-eyed Irishmen, sporting his vintage black tie and tails. The lovers toast with a glass of the bubbly. It so happens that drinks are half price till 7:30 and a free hot buffet is included at the bar.

Loading their plates with exotic fried delicacies, they indulge. The soft music makes way for the couple to share a slow dance before they head back to the bar with a light buzz and gentle talk of romance.

Dan, in his suave manner, captivates Annette as his time machine leaves the station with her heart onboard. A three-block carriage ride whisks them down Central Park South, exiting at Fifth Avenue. Surrounded by the original members of the famous New York skyline—Bonwit Teller, Tiffany's, Bergdorf's, Top of the Sixes, they pay a visit with the Lord at St. Patrick's Cathedral to light a candle and say a quick prayer. So far the meter is reading six dollars, *"the holy water is free."*

Strolling south one city block, they admire Atlas holding his globe, then on to the ice skating rink at Radio City Plaza. It's the year 1901—so far the dream perfect, just as she remembered. Her man is a magician.

Later, the couple steps down the stairwell to the old IRT Number 9 train, taking the front car next to the engineer. As the train makes its way screeching and banging through the tunnel, Dan and Annette hold hands in the dark. Sparks fly off the walls, lighting the tunnel in a display of fireworks celebrating their love.

Reaching their destination at West Canal Street, the couple makes their way through the decrepit bog of a station to the street above. Here, back in time, the buildings remain unchanged from the days of horses and wagons delivering goods to the many marketplaces that thrived there. The meat-packing district gives way to the egg and cheese markets, and the produce importers seem to have just gone home.

In these backstreet cobblestone alleyways, converted old gas lamps cast their glow on iron-shuttered windows of the ghost factories of the past. Annette remarks to Dan, "Honey, you've watched too many episodes of the *Twilight Zone*." They laugh.

Then the two take a timeless romp down lower Broadway, placing them at the Staten Island Ferry, where Dan purchases a set of round-trip tickets to the highlight event of the evening. On board, he springs for one large Coke and a pretzel. Annette dashes to the ladies room as he reserves two rear deck seats for the opening act. Tonight, blessed by a full moon, the ferry departs the slip opening the curtain to the most enchanting stage known to mankind: the New York City skyline on a clear and glorious evening.

As the ferry sails out into the harbor, the set comes alive with the grand scenery from yesteryear. The Financial District is still rich in its old-world splendor, with lamps burning deep into the evening just as in the days of the ticker tape. As the ferry reaches the center of the harbor, the Brooklyn, Manhattan, Williamsburg and 59th Street Bridges spanning the East River and the George Washington Bridge to the west on the Hudson all come into view—hanging like jewels from a necklace with the Statue of Liberty as a brilliant pendant to the Manhattan skyline. The lovers engage in a mystical dance across the rear deck of their fantasy ship.

As the music dissolves into the quiet of the evening, Dan complains to Annette, "I could have bought this island from the Indians for what this date cost."

Annette, smiles. "Well sport, I don't know about that, could you handle a twelve-dollar mortgage?"

The two laugh as they embrace silver waves with three dollars to spare.

Their love is timeless.

A SUNDAY WITH LOU

It's Sunday afternoon and the men are in the living room watching the opening game between the famed New York Giants and the home-team Philadelphia Eagles. On the mantle next to the TV, a frame showcases two brothers in their varsity football uniforms. John and James, along with their families, are here today to honor their dad, Louis James Rabino, on his sixty-fifth birthday. Lou, an Army Veteran, sits in his special recliner dressed in his usual set of standard-issue Army fatigues, circa Vietnam. Aligning next to Lou is his son-in-law, Daniel, as the two are engaged in the usual lines of defense for their favorite team in a match of armchair quarterbacking that has been played on this field for many years.

Brought up in Philadelphia, Lou has a natural distain for the New York teams and enjoys every opportunity to capitalize on the Giants' mishaps, annoying his two sons.

John, a veteran New York City policeman, and James, a veteran New York City fireman, will spend the rest of the football season here with their families in the stadium built by Lou.

The presence of grandchildren at play is apparent with the usual din of screams and cries from the kitchen. Walking into the parlor, Annette announces to the team, "Dinner is being served." The men huddle, requesting a delay. She agrees, returning to the sidelines. Back in the kitchen she helps her sisters-in-law round up and feed the children. Diane, a shapely blond, is James's wife. Jane, a brunette intellectual-type, is married to John.

Annette runs the home that was once nurtured by her mother, who passed away when Annette was eight years old. Loving and close to her dad, she has always carried out the duties of the woman of the house. Her men love and protect her, keeping their home a safe and happy place after their great loss.

Her dad, Lou, has worked thirty-four years for the same financial firm, Cantor Fitzgerald, which recently moved their headquarters to the World Trade Center. Daniel, who recently graduated Brooklyn University with a Masters in Finance, has just secured his first serious job with the help of his father-in-law at the same firm.

Annette and Daniel's marriage of two years is healthy with the usual growth spurts. Lou helps them stay on track with the wisdom he gladly shares from his happy marriage to her mom. No matter how tense the issue, he finds the right words to assure them. "Once you have a child, you won't have time for the small stuff."

At halftime, the men file into the kitchen locker room recapping the plays of the first half. The ladies, ready for the halftime show, dish out Sunday's pasta in quick haste. The children attack the men as they tackle their plates and the clock ticks to the second half. Daniel, a rookie, makes a pass at Annette while her brothers continue coaching their wives.

This is life in the Rabino family—a simple and good life!

When the game ends, the men return to the kitchen, Lou hashing out the same old excuses and accusations that led to the trouncing of his Philadelphia team.

Jane begins to pour coffee while Diane sets the table for dessert. The children are asleep. The brothers, aroused by the supreme beating given by their team, are pardoned for their illegal use of hands as their wives chuckle like schoolgirls.

Annette appears from behind the refrigerator door, surprising her dad with a big whipped cream birthday cake straight from Luigi Alba's Pastry Shop. They all join together singing to Lou. Blowing out the candles, he silently makes a wish.

Together they cheer embracing their dad with love and affection as they cut the cake and listen eagerly to Lou's birthday wish. "Well children, I know it's not my business, but I want to make a proposal."

"I'm not getting any younger…I'm sixty-six and in the fourth quarter of my life." The drama continues. "I'm a bit old-fashioned and I pray that before too long, Annette and Daniel will give us a grandchild." Sweetening the deal, he continues. "Let me lay my cards on the table. The offer is this: if you bless us with a new baby, I'll fix the third floor apartment and move you up there myself."

This triggers a heated debate on the pros and cons of starting a family so soon, when all at once the grandchildren awake from hibernation, screaming in unison, unleashing their kiddie chaos on the party. Diane and Jane immediately attend to their needs as their husbands sit oblivious. The point is moot.

Annette helps with the children as John reprimands his father for starting a riot on a peaceful Sunday afternoon. Lou, defending himself to his sidekick, Daniel, tries to drum up support for his view.

Diane and Jane, with milk bottles, rattles, dolls and blankets, eventually quiet down the kids as peace returns to the kitchen. Annette thanks her dad for his generous offer of the apartment but informs him that she will continue to work in order to help save money to buy their own home while finishing her teaching degree.

Disappointed, her dad proceeds to read the birthday cards and opens his gifts. As the day ends, the family starts packing up for their ride home. Annette's brother, John, asks if she and Daniel would be available to babysit for them the following Saturday while they attend his partner's wedding. Apologetically, Annette informs him that she and Daniel have planned a short vacation to Montauk for school break that weekend and wouldn't be available. At that moment, Lou steps in, offering to watch his grandchildren if they're dropped off at his home. It's agreed.

The family files out, leaving Annette, her dad and Daniel tidying up. She reminds her men she will be joining them for the ride into Manhattan in the morning, then kisses her dad on the cheek good night.

***

Their life is peaceful, loving and rich with
the dreams of rewards for success.
God's signs were showing them the way.

USHERING IN THE NEW YEAR

A perfect day to be alive, Annette prepares breakfast, pouring two bowls of her special high-octane oatmeal. Today she is meeting her close friend, Brenda, for breakfast in the city to discuss a potential full-time teaching position at her school.

On the way to the subway station, Dan surprises Annette with an invitation to join him for lunch at their favorite downtown restaurant, the Winter Garden, overlooking the many luxury yachts that visit the North Cove Marina, adjacent to the World Trade Towers. Annette is on a cloud.

As the train pulls into the station at Cortland Street, she hugs and kisses both her men, wishing them a good day as they do in return. Continuing uptown a short fifteen-minute ride, Annette arrives at the station at 51st and 7th. Exiting the subway, she rises to the street, her senses exploding with the energy of the city. Cutting diagonally across 7th Avenue, she heads one block north, reaching her destination, the Europa Café. Not difficult to find, as Brenda described the landmark perfectly—a carousel without wooden horses, just wooden people.

Annette is greeted by a beautiful, young female hostess with a European accent, who escorts her to a small café table situated on the southeast corner of this popular outdoor promenade, giving a clear view down 7th Avenue to Times Square. Sitting in a trance, she smiles recalling the last time she was in Times Square. It was two years ago for the New Year's Eve celebration. She remembers standing in the street amongst thousands of New Yorkers—Daniel and Annette tuning out the world as he surprised her with a diamond engagement ring. He proposed to her as the New Year's Eve Ball dropped from the tower of the Times Building, ushering in the New Year 1999. The crowd screamed as if joining them in celebration of this momentous occasion.

From her vantage point, she looks south through a maze of skyscrapers and electronic billboards, creating a bizarre video game with advertisements for Puff Daddy cologne and young females scantily dressed by Victoria's Secret. News tickers wrap the buildings, showcasing the opening numbers of the stock exchange.

Suddenly, Annette snaps out of her trance, when from the corner of her eye, the figure of a woman standing over her comes into focus. Brenda has arrived. The two women embrace in a warm gesture of friendship. Taking their seats, they immediately begin catching up on recent events in their lives.

The model-like waitress hands them menus, offering a beverage. Annette's order is interrupted by two fire trucks turning the corner with a loud, almost deafening blast of sirens. The women sit frozen as the sound passes. Annette remarks, "They can make you deaf. Let's try it again!"

The waitress smiles, focusing on her customers, trying to take their order. Once again, the stark sounds of sirens intrudes as another squad of emergency vehicles passes through. All three women look down Broadway toward Times Square. In an instant, another two fire trucks and an ambulance follow. A nervous laugh is shared as the sound dissipates. Just another typical day in New York City. Annette exclaims, "Well, excuse me! As a taxpayer of this fair city, I would like to enjoy my breakfast in peace."

At that moment, another ambulance careens around the corner. Their eyes follow it as it disappears into the canyon. The waitress makes another attempt as Brenda scrolls her finger under the breakfast item displaying two eggs any style, home fries and a toasted baguette for $6.99. The waitress looks at Annette who gestures, "The same." She nods and heads towards the kitchen.

A bit frazzled, the two hold hands and look at each other with the same nervous smile. Brenda breaks the tension by asking how Daniel is doing at his new job. As Annette begins to answer, her cell phone chirps announcing a new voice message. Her instincts go on high alert. At that moment, another wave of emergency vehicles frantically passes in a panicked display. The normal high volume of the city seems much greater today than she remembered. "How can people live this way?"

Excusing herself to retrieve her voicemail, she hears Dan's panic-stricken voice: "Honey, I'm trapped in the office!"

Then background noise overpowers as he continues: "There has been a plane crash!" A loud hiss interrupts. "Annette, I love you." The phone dies, the message ends.

Annette sits frozen, trying to make sense of Daniel's message. She pardons herself again and tries to call Daniel back. Unable to make a connection, she tries over and over as Brenda watches on. Annette repeats Daniel's message to Brenda as the women sit stunned in their first-row seats to this surreal disaster.

Yet another group of emergency vehicles, fire engines, ambulances and police cars impose their noise and confusion, driving their caravan of death through the heart of New York City. Overcome by fear, Annette stands up at the table and stares down Broadway to Times Square with a premonition that the ball of her once happy and loving life was now being dropped into a world of chaos.

In a sudden blaze of confused colors, the billboards flash in unison, displaying an emergency news bulletin replacing life as we know it. The vivid image of a jet liner crashing into one of the World Trade Towers is flashed across the many screens in a chorus line of horror. Annette screams to Brenda as she screams to the world, "How could this be happening?"

People pour onto the streets, packing into Times Square in a surreal madness, ushering in the New Year, announcing the beginning of the end...9/11 has arrived!

The noise in the city rises to an even higher level as Annette stands yelling, "I must to go to them! Daniel and my father are there! They'll need me!"

Grabbing her bag, she leaves Brenda at the table and runs to the street. At the corner, a taxi discharges a passenger; Annette dives into the back seat ordering the driver to head to the World Trade Center. The driver, a burly Middle Eastern man with a full beard and turban, pulls away from the curb in silence.

Trapped in her crusade to rescue her loved ones, she flips open her cell phone and dials Daniel's number. Again a recording! She commands the driver to take 9th Avenue. The cab turns the corner confronted with a screen displaying a jetliner hitting the second tower. Screaming at the driver, she orders him to hurry. He remains silent. Repeatedly she tries her dad's office. The phone rings with no answer.

Proceeding downtown, the taxi is rerouted as fire trucks and emergency vehicles of every kind barrel down the street toward the scene. Annette, captive in the rear seat, crying hysterically, screams out directions upon deaf ears. They reach Canal Street. A police blockade rerouting traffic is now gridlocked. She reaches into her purse and stuffs a handful of cash into the plexiglass opening. The driver remains silent.

Now commencing her journey on foot, she runs three blocks reaching the West Side Highway. Turning the corner, she finds herself blocked by a mob of people screaming in panic, blocking the sidewalk. She navigates her way through the crowd until she finds the street and suddenly stops in her tracks. She hears the screams. "They're falling! They're falling!" The vision of both towers engulfed in smoke and flames, Annette stumbles, falling across the fender of a parked car. Staring into the face of death, panic and smoke fill the air. The streets are in turmoil with people running covered in ash, terrorized. At that moment...

The first tower collapses to the ground along with Annette.

* * *

Awakening from a hellish dream in what seems to be the kitchen, or maybe living room, in the back of a Latin bodega, Annette is now surrounded by her newly adopted family. The grandmother holds her hands as the young daughter wipes the blood and soot from Annette's bruised body. The rest of the family has their eyes glued to a small, black and white television.

She tries desperately to free herself from the recurring nightmare she experienced as a child: being abandoned after the loss of her mother. This dream would engage her in its terrifying grip, where no one would see or hear her. She begs to be saved.

The old woman applies ice to the bruises on Annette's face, snapping her back to this terrifying reality blaring from the TV. A news reporter is confirming the grim details of the World Trade Center tragedy: Jet liners were used by suspected terrorists to attack the World Trade Towers. With the screen showing the entire sequence of the tragedy over and over…

Annette fades away.

SAINT VINCENT

Annette awakens in St. Vincent's Hospital emergency room with her sisters-in-law, Diane and Jane, at her bedside. She begs them frantically to explain what happened.

"You're in St. Vincent's Hospital. You passed out in the back of a store. The family called for an ambulance and they brought you here. You're alright, just try to relax."

Startled, she tries to make sense of what has happened.

"I was trying to find Dan and Dad... are they okay?"

They hold Annette closely. "Sweetheart, Dad and Daniel were killed when the towers collapsed."

"Oh no... no... they didn't get out!"

"Annette, please stay calm. We need you to be strong." Annette cries out as the horror of her loss slowly sinks in.

"Annette, our world has changed. We need you to be strong... we all have to be strong!"

Diane bursts out in tears.

"What do you mean, Diane?"

"We lost James and John." The ladies collapse onto the bed, holding each other, overwhelmed with emotion.

"What are you saying? Oh my God! What has happened?"

"They were called to the emergency. When the buildings collapsed, they were trapped in the stairway."

Annette shuts her eyes as if to hide from the horror and slips away again.

The nurse is summoned.

39

THE DEPARTED

The souls of the departed are led in a procession
by the messengers of the Almighty.
They have risen from this world of flesh
and have become one with the universe.

Those left behind are damaged and cannot
comprehend this horrendous loss.

We on Earth are helpless to join them
in their beautiful flight to the heavens,
and are saddened.

Their souls, too rich to remain trapped
in this material world.
They were never meant to visit for long.

May we be convinced that even before
we reach up to God,
Thou art reaching down to us.

THE PROPHECY

Today, 9/11, we stand witness as the clock has begun ticking to the Mayan prophecy of 2012, the alignment of planets shifting the axis of world dominance.

Our world has been thrown into chaos in the rude awakening of the twenty-first century, draining the power of once mighty nations into the veins of new lands. The word of God has been distorted by the corruption of nations and one man to another. The antichrist has arrived. He is the defective byproduct of the Western world. He has amassed armies who have lain dormant for centuries leading to this great prophecy. His lobby has touched every soul that walks on this sacred ground we call Earth. The members of nations no longer believe in their nations. Corruption spews from the vents of a once great society, the air poisoned with scandal.

The fallout shelters of the Cold War now transcend to space exploration, desperately seeking to propagate our values on alien nations of the universe…leaving behind a bleeding planet. Yet they have failed to respect the humble microcosms of mankind that will bring this civilization to its knees.

* * *

The morning is bright and still, just like the morning Annette's family was stolen from her in the terrorist act of 9/11. A rifle detachment marches onto the field honoring a dead brother, Sergeant Louis Ernesto Rabino. Four coffins are lined together, creating a landscape of disbelief to a small, loving family and compassionate onlookers. A bugler plays taps as the sounds of rifles pierce the morning air with a grim reminder that death has reached their doorstep.

Annette, her sisters-in-law, their children and Daniel's widowed mother huddle together to console each other amidst this horror. As the priest reads scripture, the sound of a large jetliner flies overhead, announcing the return of life "Back to Normal."

Annette turns inward in prayer and reflection. Could there be a greater loss…one as complete as this…one so perfectly aimed at her life and the life of her loved ones?

The caskets descend.

THE DARK OF WINTER

It's late fall nearing Thanksgiving 2001. Annette has been wrapped safely in the shelter of her home. The days are becoming ever shorter as autumn passes into the darkness of winter. Avoiding phone calls and discarding mail from the survivors' support groups, Annette isolates herself, embracing her despair.

Having quit her substitute teaching job, she sits home disconnected from the outside world. Small projects around the house have become monumental tasks, inhibited by a numbness that has taken over her being. The traditional Sunday family dinner that brought the house alive with love and purpose is gone forever, leaving only the ghost of a life past.

Annette falls deeper and deeper into despair with each passing day. Occasionally visiting her nieces and nephews, she momentarily finds solace in a world that makes no sense. Her sisters-in-law seemed to have better adjusted to this new life of loss, as they remain active and alert to their children and the world at large. Lost and alone, she survives another day on the love they share and the memories deep in her heart.

The vacation plans she and Daniel had for their annual trip to Montauk have come and gone with no break in sight, just the daily torment of loneliness. Unable to pray, she wrestles with the feeling that God has trapped her, persecuted in a Hell on Earth by stripping away all her dreams and the desires to fulfill them.

"How could anything of value come of this? Where is the lesson learned for the price paid? How does someone see a better tomorrow when today is so dark and void of promise? What does a person do to deserve this? Why did my beautiful men leave this Earth?"

* * *

The phone rings, she answers—another reporter looking for an interview with the survivor of the greatest tragedy of 9/11.

Annette declines.

A YEAR IN TURMOIL

In the years following his greatest legal triumph, Joe finds himself sinking out of touch with his profession and practice. With clients few and far between, he picks up mostly misdemeanor cases from young transients and surfers out at The End, most unable to pay for the services rendered.

Heavily involved in the anti-war movement and making an attempt to break into local politics, he lives out an almost reclusive existence. He distances himself from friends, his practice, his marriage, his life. Days spent out in Montauk surfing provide a refuge while he helplessly falls from the perch of the success he once knew.

In Vicky's witness to Joe's collapse and concern over their financial condition, she quietly contemplates selling their beach home. Setting a meeting with a local realtor creates even more stress on an already fragile marriage. The couple's only remaining bond exists in their two sons, Vincent and Joe Jr.

Vincent, training at the Marine Corp Officers Candidate School, is soon to graduate and slated to serve his first combat tour in Iraq. Helplessly, they watch Joe Jr., Joe's son from a previous marriage, sink into further depression.

On sleepless nights, Vicky prays that Vincent does not become another living casualty of war like his dad. At night, Joe wrestles with his demons. Reliving past horrors, tormented by the faces of the Marines who died while serving under his command, the burden weighs heavily on his soul for failing to keep them alive.

How could a mortal take on such a faithful task?
Would God dare to do so?

Unable to shake this parasite that lives deep within, he falls deeper and deeper into darkness. Vicky, unable to reach accord with Joe's form of dementia, sets her life in another direction. Working longer hours at her job, she secures a long-awaited promotion. On most weekends, she stays in the city, only occasionally visiting the beach house.

In the months ahead, Joe tries to salvage the skeleton of a still-failing practice. Working through the long hours of the evening writing his memoirs mainly about life and war, he fills his days surfing. Vicky and Joe worlds apart, their once marriage of plenty now starves like a fragile plant hidden in the back of a dark closet waiting to be fed.

On weekends, Joe looks forward to his visits from Joe Jr., who arrives on the 5 p.m. train from Brooklyn. His son, now 32, is deeply afflicted with a bipolar disorder and on several occasions has attempted to take his life. For the first time as father and son, a bond is shared between the two, filling an emotional gap to their lonely existence.

In early spring at the request of his wife, Joe pays a visit to the city to Dr. Ronald Gold, Psychotherapist, for an exploratory session intended to identify the pain that has caused him to withdraw from life.

Ron, an old school buddy and surf brother, is a close friend of the family. The two share much history, having roomed together at Fordham University back in the '60s.

Ron and Joe embrace in a brotherly show of affection. "Joe, come on in. Have a seat."

"Ron, where were you Sunday? The surf was epic! Vic and I got to the ditch early before the crowds."

"Nah, I couldn't make it," Ron sighs. "I'm juggling more balls than a one-arm paper hanger. Actually we were meeting with the caterer for my daughter Marissa's Sweet Sixteen, which we expect you and Vicky to attend.

"We'll be there, don't worry."

"How's Vicky?"

"She's doing fine… mostly staying in the city… still working and just got a promotion…. Ron, how is Donna feeling?"

"She's good. We had a little scare but we're okay now. We plan on taking the whole family to the Bahamas next month."

Ron catches Joe staring into space. "How are the boys doing?"

Joe snaps out of his trance. "Oh, they're doing fine…. Vincent is wrapping up his Officers training at Quantico next month and then ships out to Iraq for his first tour of duty."

"You must be real proud of him, a chip off the old block and a hard charger like his dad!"

"Well… I guess in some ways he is."

"If he takes after you, Joe, he's an achiever."

"Yeah… but Vicky isn't happy about Vincent joining the Marines. It scares her."

"Well, I understand. As a mother she's afraid for her son's well-being."

"I know… but maybe she's afraid he'll turn out like me, frozen in time."

"Joe, I'm sorry to say you look troubled. I've never seen you this way."

"I'm fine, Ron. My son Joe and I are spending some quality time together out at the beach house… it's been good."

"So, how are you and Vicky doing?"

"We're okay… like I said, she spends most of her time in the city. She's happy there and I've been staying mostly out on the island. We speak at least once a week."

"Joe, Vicky says you're stuck. All you talk about is the Nam while life is passing you by."

"I know, Ron… it's a tough time. The practice is slow, but I'm trying to make things happen… we'll get by."

"Joe, you have always been my idol! We all looked up to you, All-City Wrestler, graduated Fordham Law first in your class! Great with the ladies…and if it weren't for you, I would never have met Donna."

"Yeah, that was cool."

"Cool….you call that cool? Why you invented cool! We had never even seen a surfboard until you showed up at the beach in your flowered jams…now that was cool! I remember the summer before you joined the Marines, lifeguarding at Rockaway Beach. Tan, muscular… no wonder you were so popular with the girls. I remember Doris just had to have you for herself. She even conned you into marrying her before you shipped out."

"Ron, she was pregnant."

"Yeah, but you guys looked great together. What happened? You're a hero."

"A hero? I was no hero! We made no difference... we were treated like murderers!"

"Joe, don't say that, none of us had the balls to go to that war."

Joe is now aroused from his usual soft demeanor. "Balls, you call it balls...it was crazy. I came back from the Nam to less than a hero's welcome. I wore my uniform proudly—my life, my identity was that of a Marine. It's all we had.

We came home proud, but we were shunned. I came home to find my friends, even my family, divided as to what I stood for. I thought that war served a purpose for our country and this world."

"Joe, why do you feel that way?"

Taking a deep breath, Joe continues, "We came to understand a terrible truth, that the lives and limbs sacrificed by my brothers stood for nothing in the eyes of the American people. All the death that drove a stake through the hearts and souls of these brave men, leaving their families crippled back home, was just a waste of good life, forgotten forever like a bad memory.

"But how could that be? We were so proud you."

"Ron, I remember on the flight home I imagined I would

be met at the airport by Doris, my family, or at least my friends.... No one was there. Just the faces of strangers with cold stares piercing through me with fear and contempt. During the taxi ride home, I remember being afraid and insecure that I didn't fit in anymore.

"Doris hadn't written me in over three months. I was afraid of what I was going to find and wondered if she still loved me. I surprised her, standing proud in my uniform. She came to the door holding my newborn son. Staring at me, she broke out laughing and said I looked like a clown. Then she invited me into my own home like an unwelcome stranger. She hands me my son while keeping her distance and informs me that she is going out with Steven Sapia. Then she asks me to remove my belongings that were packed into four boxes lying near the door. That's when it hit me: the war was not over.

"I had to defend myself every day. I stopped wearing my uniform around the neighborhood because it just brought on to much controversy. The only time I did dress was on my visits to the USO Club at Fort Hamilton. The only place I felt comfortable was with my brothers. I could relate to them. As a matter of fact, until you visited me on your school break, I stayed home alone at my parents' house, feeling out of place but at least able to get by with their love and support. Ron, we weren't heroes, we were freaks, we were outcasts and we still are. No one wants to hear our stories.

"Even Vicky made me promise to stop talking about the

Nam when she's around. I live my life with those memories and can't get free of them. Sometimes they haunt me and ironically sometimes they make me feel safe."

Ron is saddened by the weight Joe still carries from the war—a heavier burden today than he ever realized. He sees Joe stuck in this helpless funk, his age ever apparent through a gray unshaven face and war-torn eyes deeply recessed in their sockets. A hard question flashes across Ron's mind:

What can we do to save our friend?
A real friend, a friend in need.
Is there a fix, a remedy for a soul
so severely damaged?
So many have gone before him,
So few have made it this far.
Can I make a difference?

Ron stands, walks over to Joe and pulls him from his chair, hugging his buddy. "Joe, I feel your pain. There must be a way out of this…at least we can try to find one. Just remember one thing: the smaller the surf, the longer the board."

Joe looks at Ron inquisitively, breaking the tension with a good, hard laugh as Ron continues.

"Joe, you know you have always been the fixer and now it's my turn, so let's wax up and hit the surf."

Amused, Joe remarks, "I like that."

"The reason you're here is to get you unstuck, as Vicky

calls it. So we're going to have to get creative, just like riding a wave. We both know you like to write. You've already published four stories, so where can we go with this?"

"Well, I have been writing my memoirs and want to compile them to create a book."

"Joe, that sounds admirable but will you make it in time to feed the family?"

Joe shrugs, shaking his head side to side.

"You have a law degree and bachelors in social science. So here's an idea…let me make a call to a close buddy of mine, Dean Gray, at NYU. I think you met him out at the ditch. Just maybe he can hook you up with a part-time teaching position. How would you like that? A job where you can utilize your writing skills and life's experience to enlighten our youth with a finer appreciation for their freedom. And get paid for doing it!"

"Well, I'll guess I'll give it a try."

"Okay, then send me a copy of your resume and let's get started."

Ron and Joe shake hands.

***

Two weeks later, a letter arrives from the Dean of Social Sciences at New York University, offering Joe a teaching position for the upcoming summer semester of 2002.

With a hand from the heavens, Joe accepts.

THE WINTER FROST

Winter has arrived. Annette sits gazing out the frost-covered window of her garden apartment at the children playing in the snow. She wonders why she ever quit her teaching job and left the lovely little people she was so fond of. She and Dan were planning their very own family before he was stolen from her on that fateful day. At night, she lies in bed waiting for her belly to start twitching with the new life that would have connected her and Dan for eternity.

Spending endless days at home, captive in her mind, unable to join the outside world, she sits alone and abandoned trying to establish a purpose for her existence. She is unable to engage with any form of media, which is riddled with the news of the World Trade disaster and the search for the villains of 9/11, that at last report were dragging our nation into a senseless war with senseless people. Disappointed with the circus of fools that has prevailed from this tragedy, she thinks, "If nations were only responsible to their people, none of this would have taken place. We would not be the enemy and I would have my family back!"

The winter of 2002 is cold and dark in her heart. Few times does Annette venture from her home, shying away from friends and neighbors, merely existing. Her friend, Brenda, visits most weekends, finding Annette frozen in time, unable to open up and return to the relationship they so enjoyed. Long discussions now seem to take them back to the same dead end with no future. Lovingly frustrated and unwilling to see Annette destroy her life with grief, Brenda takes a stand. Removing a notebook from her bag, she opens it up to an empty page and lays it out before Annette.

"Here, my friend, is where you are. It's a blank canvas called the present. You see it is bright and clear, open for your interpretation. I don't see any death and destruction there, do you?"

Annette looks at Brenda somewhat shocked and amused.

"I am giving you a new life with this notebook. Every day you must create a new page and begin with a new attitude if you are to go on living in this world...and that, my dear, is the only option! Sink your teeth back into life before you starve from malnutrition of the spirit.

"You will report to me every week until I promote you back into the world of the living. Do you understand!?"

Annette, for the first time since that terrible day, raises her head and opens her heart, embracing Brenda and the promise of a new life.

"To start, write down on your calendar: I will return to school to get my master's degree so I can apply for the teaching position at New York High."

Taking the pen from Brenda, Annette stares down at the open page of the notebook.

She makes the entry.

A CROSS TO BEAR

0600hrs – Joe slips on a pair of sweatpants and heads for the kitchen. Cody, the Chesapeake lab, follows behind him. Leading him out back, Mr. Hoggs, a big tomcat, comes in from his nightly rampage.

Filling their bowls, he walks over to the stove and heats up a pot of coffee before heading back upstairs.

Setting the shower, he prepares for his five-minute drill, a routine embedded since Marine Corps Boot Camp. Lathering his face for a one-minute shave, he trims his sideburns on an angle, brushes his teeth and steps into the shower for a quick soaping followed by a rinse and a towel dry. Reaching into the overstuffed closet, he removes a set of freshly starched Marine Corps combat fatigues. When he places them on the bed, Vicky stirs, glancing at Joe.

Rummaging inside the closet through a myriad of shoes, sandals and sneakers, he retrieves a spit-shined pair of combat boots. Now dressed, he returns to the kitchen. Sipping a cup of coffee, he turns on the radio to a local surf report:

Brisk winds coming out of the north at 10 to 15 mph, water temperature 50 degrees, air temperature 55 degrees, high tide..............................

As he stares out the window, his mind wanders to a reflection in time of an overcast morning where the gray mist hugged the earth.

* * *

Only four weeks In Country, Delta company is moving northwest through a steady drizzle. They are in a combat column. Delta One is point, Joe follows with Delta Three and Captain Hendricks is with Delta Two in the rear out of sight.

It is mid-morning when the drizzle stops. Delta One moves onto the crest of a small hill. There is a village across a large stream to their left. He is just starting up the hill with his platoon...Boom! Boom! They duck... freezing as large pieces of gray shrapnel spin to his left, taking down three of his men. He sees several villagers running, guilty knowledge taking flight: Delta One has hit two land mines. The sound of heavy rifle fire fills the air. Grenades exploding from the crest of the hill, the cries come: "Corpsman up, Corpsman up!"

The racket continues for ten minutes. They're pinned down as desperate cries for help come across the radio. Then a barrage of mortar rounds explodes, echoing the horror through the valley...

Joe yells down the line to his Marines, "Stay in place, face outboard, this is an ambush!" He can't see the crest and can't move up to take a look or else risk setting off other mines.

His radio operator says Delta Six wants to speak to him. "Delta Six, Delta Three actual, over."

"Lieutenant, move up to Delta One immediately, give me a situation report, out!"

"Yes Sir, out!"

Damn! Why can't Delta One Actual give Six a situation report?

He tells his R.O. to stay put! He'll use Delta One's radio. He starts to ascend, looking for hidden wires as well as rocks or broken branches arranged in unnatural patterns. Carefully looking down at each step he takes, he slowly moves up reaching the crest.

"The situation to my right...a number of Marines down. Delta One Actual is standing off to my left, facing away."

Joe approaches one of his men. "Rob." No response. He continues to face away. "Rob." Still no response. As Joe grabs his left shoulder, Rob turns to him, tears streaking his soiled face.

"Joe, I can't do this anymore. I won't take them one more step."

Rob falls to his knees, wraps his arms around Joe's legs and rests his head against his stomach. Holding him firmly, Joe bows his head with tears creasing his own dirty face as his R.O. approaches.

"Delta Six wants to speak to Lieutenant Giannini."

He raises Rob to his feet and takes the handset.

"Delta Six, this is Delta Three Actual, over."

"Lieutenant, what's going on up there? Over."

"We're in a mine field, seventeen priorities, over."

"Lieutenant, what do you suggest? Over."

"We can't go forward. Get Slicks to lift us out of here, over."

"I can't get Slicks, over."

"Then we'll have to retrace our steps. We might be walking into another ambush, over."

"Medevacs are on the way. Let me know when the wounded are onboard, Six Out!"

"Yes sir, out!"

"Rob, get your men ready to load the wounded onto Medevacs. We're moving off this hill! Your platoon will be tail-end Charlie."

Rob nods and walks slowly into the midst of the downed Marines.

Joe turns, moving cautiously to the nearest one lying prone on his poncho at a slight incline, his head tilted back. He's calm—the morphine has kicked in. Kneeling down beside his right shoulder facing his lower body, Joe sees the Marine's jungle trousers have been mostly blown away, each leg an abstract color, torn slabs of white grizzle, red muscle and broken protruding bones. He says to himself, "This isn't real, it's plastic and rubber." An attempt to suppress his emotions, control getting sick: "Marine, you'll be off this hill shortly on your way back to the world."

"Sir, can I have some water?" Joe looks him over to make sure he doesn't have any stomach or belly wounds, then removes his canteen from his web belt and unscrews the cap. The wounded man remains calm; his head still tilted back. Joe slowly pours water through his slightly parted lips.

"What's your name, Marine?"

"Bell, Sir...Corporal Bell."

"Where are you from, Bell?"

"Ocean City, Maryland, Sir."

A whomping sound to the east, Joe looks up, Medevacs approaching fast.

"Bell, the Medevacs are coming in, hold tight, we'll be moving you, O.K.?"

"O.K., Sir."

The first Medevac swoops down to the hill and hovers about three feet off the ground, trying not to set off other mines. He suppresses his fear. They have to move. Bell is the furthest from the chopper; he'll be the last one out. Four-man teams carry each stretcher onto the hovering choppers, rising fast.

More choppers come in, hovering over the same spot as more wounded are carried over, then lifted aboard. The sound of small arms fire resumes from across the hill, then all hell breaks loose. They pick up Bell his head still back. He remains calm. They run toward the Medevac, lifting him aboard...his head goes forward, and then falls back. His eyes are now locked wide open, blood draining from his face, he's turning white...saw his mangled legs...he is going into shock. The chopper rises in a swirl of dust with its 50mm machine guns ablaze.

As the chopper rises over the crest, a sudden shockwave

levitates their bodies off the ground. On the horizon, the last chopper, blown from the sky, is disintegrated into smoke and ash, crashing into the treetops in a horrendous mass of flames. Corporal Bell never had a chance, a brave young man doomed. The dead and wounded have now been medevaced off the hill.

A barrage of mortar shells, snaps him back as they are pinned down in a minefield, taking on heavy casualties.

Today we lost twenty-seven Marines,
the end of a dream.

* * *

Kneeling on the soft, soaked grass of the churchyard, hammering a white cross into the earth, Joe and his Marines are on a mission to erect three hundred crosses in honor of the Veterans Day Memorial Service at First Presbyterian Church in the town of East Hampton, New York.

Today there will be no surf.

CONNECTION WITH THE PAST

Annette is filing through a stack of house bills when the phone rings. A real estate agent in the neighborhood wants to show her clients her dad's apartment. Asking for a few extra minutes to tidy up, she agrees.

Stacking the bills and placing them in the drawer of the oak roll-top desk, she notices her application for evening class still sitting there. Annette places it on the kitchen table, closes the door and climbs a flight of stairs that leads to the parlor floor apartment. Rarely visiting her father's apartment since her loss, she is hesitant and afraid to stir the memories that lie within.

Entering, she turns on the light to this time capsule, taking in the unique fragrance that comprises the many fabrics that created the cloth of their family. Curtains, sofa, sitting chairs and a large Persian rug contribute to this bouquet of a time past.

Among the photos that line the fireplace mantel is one of her and Daniel standing on the front steps on their wedding day, thinking fondly of the dreams they shared to one day raise a family in a brownstone of their own. She glances at the photos of her brothers in their dress uniforms on graduation day from the Police and Fire Academies, remembering how proud they were to have accomplished their training. Then, she spots a picture she had always admired while growing up of her dad dressed in his Army uniform, garnished in medals and ribbons, awarded him for his campaigns in the Vietnam War.

Looking down, she notices the family album her dad kept on the cocktail table in front of the sofa. Opening to the first photo of her brothers and their new families posing in front of the Christmas tree, dated December 25, 1998. Turning the pages, she witnesses the grandchildren growing up into the little people they are today, a dim reminder that her brothers will never see them reach their dreams.

Randomly, she places her finger into the center of the album, flipping open to a photo of her mom holding her as a baby, bringing on a pang to her maternal instincts. She loses track of time, viewing more photos of the annual family vacations in Montauk with her brothers posing in front of the lighthouse and one of her parents holding hands on the beach. How long ago it seems. Then a small index card falls to the floor. Picking it up Annette reads a recipe:

Enchanted Evening

Meeting Spot: Charlie's Clam Bar
½ price drinks, free hors d'oeuvres and tip $5.00
Carriage ride – three blocks $5.00
Light one candle at Saint Patrick's Cathedral $1.00
Holy Water Free
Two Fares IRT #9 Subway to Canal Street $1.20
Two Fares, Staten Island Ferry Roundtrip $2.00
1 Pretzel and a Coke $1.30 (Coke optional)

She smiles, realizing these were the ingredients that Daniel used in the potion that won her love.

Just then, the doorbell rings. Placing the card back, Annette closes the album and composes herself before opening the front door. The agent apologizes for the short notice, introducing a pleasant young couple in their late twenties or early thirties.

Both are overwhelmed as they take their first look at this authentic, turn-of-the-century brownstone apartment nestled in the Cobble Hill section of Brooklyn. The agent boasts to the couple, "Well, you wanted a feeling of old-world charm…this time machine is it!" Their laughter fills the room.

The floors are set in rich, golden oak parquet detailed with a cherry-wood border. Plaster ceilings with detailed borders surround an ornate center medallion. The gas-converted brass chandelier with etched glass cups perfectly encapsulates the period. Next to the bold wooden fireplace mantle, a set of brass sconces remain in their original position mounted atop the beautifully weathered wainscotting wall covering, bringing this setting to its original grandeur. As Annette leads her guests down the long hallway, the couple suddenly stops, as the young woman breaks the silence.

"Oh my God! Look at this bathroom, it's original!"

Her husband replies, "Amazing! Like the day it was built!"

Stepping inside, he walks over to the oak-mounted toilet box, asking Annette if he could try a flush. She agrees. The young man pulls on a white enamel handle, initiating a chain of events that have endured the test of time. They watch in amazement as the box sends a rush of water cascading down the pipe, flushing the toilet below. He then turns to his wife. "Dear, I'm sold. This is the one!"

The group proceeds to the master bedroom, where they are fascinated by a bold, tarnished brass bed exemplifying its character and strength. A large Victorian armoire stands catty-corner, sharing the same rich carvings as the dresser against the adjacent wall.

At the head of the room, facing the street, are three large bay windows, framing dark wooden shutters that help filter the outside world. On the cornice above, beautiful panels of stained lead glass windows softly cast a glow of many hues. The couple quietly asks the agent to put in an offer for a one-year lease.

Making their way back to the kitchen, they sit around an oak, lion-claw pedestal table and discuss the terms. Annette, feeling somewhat removed, can't believe this is happening. Looking up, she becomes lost in the intricate pattern of the tin ceiling that mirrors a black and white French-tile floor. She agrees to the terms. The agent and her clients warmly hug Annette, thanking her for being so kind, and make their way to the front door.

Peering through the lace curtains at her new tenants as they descend to the street, she realizes…

> The dreams she held in her heart,
> for now, will be shared by others.

AN OFFICER AND A GENTLEMAN

The days are closing down on the end of winter. Early on a Friday morning, Joe and Vicky pack their suitcases into the trunk of their Volvo station wagon parked outside their brownstone on West 76th Street. Somewhat awkward, the two have not been together for most of the New Year, but are now embarking on their long-awaited trip to witness the graduation of their son Vincent at the Marine Corps Officer Training School in Quantico, Virginia.

The eight-hour ride is surprisingly relaxed, reminiscing over the good times they spent as a family out at the beach house and how their sons developed over the years. How quickly life has brought them to this day.

As they make their passage to the hotel, Vicky can't help but stare at Joe, handsome, tan, always looking fit, dressed in a dark brown corduroy blazer, covering a tan turtleneck sweater. Joe is doing his best to maintain his decorum to Vicky's new look, in her sexy navy blue sweater dress. The stage is set for the revival of a relationship buried deeply in sediment of dysfunction now cleared away. The hotel room door shuts behind them, and in a sweep of primal passion, Joe and Vicky become one.

The next morning after breakfast, they arrive at the Officer Training Center. They are greeted at the gate by a handsome black sergeant giving them directions to the parade ground where the graduation ceremony will take place. After

Joe parks the car, they walk directly to the bleacher seats adjacent to the Battalion Headquarters at the far end of the parade ground.

It has been thirty-three years since Joe attended the very same ceremony as a graduate himself. Rejoicing in the excitement of his accomplishment were his parents and the same pride present here today. The core of this family stands strong and proud, loving and supportive, able to stand up to life's battles.

Today their son takes a great step in life, a step many dare not take. He is now a Marine trained for battle, trained to kill an opposing enemy, the dream of civilization now fulfilled. Vicky reaches into her purse for a tissue to wipe her eyes as her son and his platoon of brothers pass in review.

Vincent is now a graduate and an Officer in the United States Marine Corps. He glows with the same pride and accomplishment as his dad and the brothers who served under him in the Vietnam War.

A photograph is taken with his parents at his side. Vincent Giannini, an Officer and a gentleman in his Dress Blue Uniform, is announced as they enter the Officers' Dining Room.

> Today, life is full and complete,
> fortified by love and purpose
> with no obstacles in his path,
> only objectives.

A SOCIAL REGISTER

Annette arrives at the New York University Study Center opposite Washington Square Park between 10th Street and University Place.

It's been ten months since she last set foot in this city and is amazed to see the calm, almost casual life that has returned to these once devastated streets.

The campus bustles with the diverse culture of students that has made this university a renowned educational melting pot. Finally, Annette's long-awaited attempt to sign up for the final classes that will secure her a master's degree in education has arrived. She joins the crowds of students and faculty to register in this fall semester of 2002, only eight credits shy of her degree. She must decide on three classes, two of them being electives.

Heading to a table where a group of young ladies are seductively dressed in black body suits, she connects with a class designated Yoga/Pilates. Feeling relieved, she registers, thinking how healthy that class will be. Scanning the many departments, the second choice becomes a bit more difficult. Reaching into her bag, she retrieves the new semester's curriculum. After reviewing the many classes in alphabetical order, she becomes further lost.

Scrolling to the end, a class catches her eye, a subject appearing in the middle of the last page: Home Economics. The listing is accompanied by a photo of a female professor and a student repairing a leaky faucet. Annette smiles, feeling blessed to have stumbled across such a practical class for a single woman responsible for an old, needy brownstone. She makes her way to the table for the Home Economics Department and registers.

Exhausted by this first encounter with the real world, she heads toward the mezzanine level, where the student lounge and coffee machine resides. Taking two quarters from her purse, she places them into the vending machine and presses the buttons, selecting coffee with cream. Searching the crowded room for a quiet spot to indulge, she finds herself walking through the lounge area and down the hall coming to a room marked Reading Hall. She spots an easel:

<u>Reading</u>
Social Science Department, 7:30 p.m.
Professor Joseph Giannini
"The Crimes Of An Unjust War"

Intrigued, she sips her coffee and stares in wonder as the room fills in. Drawn by her instinct and curiosity, she takes the remaining seat in the last row. At the speaker podium, a handsome, middle-aged man prepares for his reading. The professor introduces himself to the audience, who has come to know him for his strong, conscientious position on government and the war machine.

After a brief dissertation on his latest work, he reads to the group. Annette listens, thinking of her dad and the many heated family discussions over this same material. Amazed, the audience sits quietly riveted on his concepts and observations dating back to pre-modern day warfare. Looking down to her left, she notices a small printed invitation lying on her neighbor's lap: it is clearly a photo of the professor in his combat gear. The inscription reads:

Marine Corps Captain
Professor Joseph A. Gianinni, Esquire
Author and Vietnam Veteran
Invites you to join him on an upcoming field trip over
Labor Day Weekend to the Vietnam War Memorial
in Washington, D.C.

Annette, now realizing the connection to her dad, immerses herself in his reading. Ending his story in what seems to be his signature short prayer, the room remains hanging on his every word as the students stand and applaud before filing out of the small auditorium.

Inspired by the words of a real true war hero, Annette makes her way to the podium, awaiting her turn to meet this great speaker. After introducing herself, she inquires about signing up for his writing class and the upcoming field trip. Relieved and triumphant in her first encounter with the new world, she takes the last sip of her cold coffee and savors the moment. She makes a brief stop in the Registrar's Office.

Her mission accomplished.

MY FRIENDS ON THE WALL

It's Labor Day Weekend, the day of the class trip to the Vietnam Memorial Wall.

Saturday, 6 AM: Sitting at the counter of a coffee shop on the corner of 49th Street and 9th Avenue, Joe waits for his students to arrive. Picking up his cell phone, he dials the bus driver to confirm the ETA as the bus makes its way in from Queens.

Students start arriving in drips and drabs, barely coherent from the events of the night before. Annette arrives quiet and alert. Taking a stool at the counter, she orders coffee and toasted bagel with cream cheese. When the microbus arrives out front, Joe pardons himself and approaches the driver as the students pay their tabs.

In typical Marine Corps procedure, Joe takes roll call as his students file onto the bus. Annette, last out of the restaurant, climbs aboard to find only two available seats adjacent to the driver in the first row. She chooses the window.

Bringing up the rear, Joe sits next to Annette and gives the bus driver a thumbs up as the bus pulls away from the curb heading south on 9th Avenue to the Lincoln Tunnel. Exiting on the Jersey side, the bus windows face Manhattan to the full view of the downtown skyline, now missing the signature twin towers like a beautiful smile missing its two front teeth from a sucker-punch brawl. All on board ride in silence as the bus makes its way to the New Jersey Turnpike.

73

Joe gives a brief run through on the day's itinerary as they settle in for the five-hour ride to D.C.

Annette, staring straight at the road ahead, wonders why there isn't a memorial for soldiers like her dad who survived that horrific war but continued to live it every day.

Joe reaches into his knapsack, removing a small, worn spiral notebook titled "Lost Brothers." Placing it on his lap catches Annette's attention.

Turning to Annette, Joe asks her if she knew anyone who fought in the Vietnam War. Briefly lost in her thoughts, she replies, "Yes, my dad fought in Vietnam. He was a Sergeant in the 182nd Airborne Division."

Joe is taken by surprise. Not expecting a connection, he asks, "Did your father speak much of the war?"

"Living with him was a constant reminder of that horrible place. He lived it his whole life and it drove my brothers crazy. Our home life was one big regiment. He always wore his fatigues around the house—that was my dad, Staff Sergeant Louis Rabino. Don't get me wrong, we loved him and understood his pain…he was just stuck in it his whole life."

Joe, now realizing he is in the presence of a member of the brotherhood of Vietnam Veterans, sits in a trance as Annette has unwittingly exposed his own life, probably the same views his family would share about himself. With a warm, gentle smile, he tells Annette, "If he were here, I would gladly give my seat for the honor of having him join us."

"Well, that's kind of you, Mr. Giannini. If he were alive, he would have accepted your gracious invitation, I'm sure. He did make trips to the Memorial with his buddies from time to time."

Joe asks Annette, "How did he die?"

Annette's eyes tear up. "Well, I'll try my best…it all happened on September 11th, 2001. My dad and my husband Dan were at work, Cantor Fitzgerald on the 101st floor of Tower 1…. I'm sure you know the rest." Trying to hold back her tears, she continues, "I know the war took so many more lives, yet the pain of September 11th is still the same."

Joe sits silent. The only sounds are that of the road as the bus passes by Baltimore Stadium. He is suddenly in touch with unusually hard-to-reach emotions buried in recollections of war and death that are now awakened. Joe and Annette are about to share a dark ride through their black box of life.

"Annette, you spend a whole lifetime avoiding death for you, for your loved ones, for people you don't even know. Some are not so fortunate…they meet death early on. They learn at a young age to accept this world of fate. They never had a choice. Some of us, considered 'the lucky ones,' live a life free of this despair, but in reality live a life in fear. Fear of loss, a shadow to living truly free—but here you have a choice. Here, life becomes mysterious: a God that grants life no longer protects us. How could this be? If He can help us win games, how could He turn a cold shoulder to us at a time of life and death?"

What kind of God could be so frivolous?

Listening to Joe carry on about life and death and God, she clears the tears from her eyes and listens like a child being read a fairytale. He continues, "I carried this dream to Vietnam, a dream that the war was just and that we could make a difference. Well, that was short lived. It took only twenty-seven days In Country for that fantasy to tumble down on my life and my Marines. In one day, in one cursed mission, my dream and my belief in that war died, along with the heroes serving under me.

There could be no sense made of it, no conciliation or humanitarian benefit derived. It was just a suicide mission ordered by people who represented a people who had no idea what damage was being placed on an innocent generation of young people. I fought for twelve more months, not believing in the principle or purpose of that war, which to me was a fate worse than death itself."

The bus arrives at Memorial Park. Joe gathers the group, handing out guides to the park. Flipping through the pages of a map, they now find themselves surrounded by monuments of man's inhumanity to man. The World War II Memorial, the Korean War Veterans Memorial, the Vietnam Memorial Wall and directly to the east, adjacent to the Washington Monument, the Holocaust Memorial Museum resides.

They find themselves standing
in the Corridor of Death.

The group steps toward the Lincoln Memorial on their journey to the wall. Making a brief stop at the foot of the Reflection Pool, Joe asks that they remain silent for a prayer.

Dear God,
Today we are here to honor the young, gentle heroes
who have died serving our nation.
Take time to reflect when men decide and
feel safe to call war insane;
Take a moment to embrace those
you have left behind.
God Bless their souls.

Amidst the confusion of crowds, the group remains intent on his words, the raw reality hitting home...it is overwhelming. He closes his notebook, thanking them for having the courage and compassion to make this journey. He leaves them with one last reminder, that this Memorial is a place for healing and to quietly rejoice in the valor and honor of these heroes. With that, the group disperses across the park lawn to the wall.

Filing through the pages of his notebook, Joe finds Annette standing in front of him as if waiting for his attention. He apologizes, inviting her to join him to visit some old friends. Removing a pad from her purse with six names, she obliges. Two hours later, the two had visited and honored ninety-five friends on the wall. Finding a bench, they rest, sharing a couple of bottles of spring-fed water and reflecting on the grotesque waste of good life that surrounds them.

Annette asks Joe how he kept track of all those men who served with him and lost their lives. Smiling, he gently slides the old "Lost Brothers" notebook across her lap, warning her, "There are some obscene details in these pages. Please be careful."

Annette cautiously opens the book to a full front view of Joe, bare-chested, a young surfer's physique, looking like a movie character with an M16 rifle slung across his torso. Photo dated July 15, 1967. On the next few pages, she encounters more photos of Joe and his Marines out in the field, looking more like buddies on a hunting expedition to some exotic jungle, maybe Africa or the Amazon. There is one of Joe surrounded by his buddies on furlough at China Beach, Vietnam, a military outpost and surf camp located in the combat zone on the China Sea. Smiling in the sun of delight, at home with his brothers, Joe will never look back. Turning through the pages Annette stumbles over some odd entries, notes, even a silly poem, then stops abruptly to an entry dated 11, August 1967.

Today B Company took significant casualties ambushed while caught in a minefield. We lost our company leader and 27 Marines, KIA (killed in action).

The page is blurred, stained by the tears shed over the fresh ink as Joe entered the names and ranks of his dead comrades.

Annette, stuck on the page...afraid to read further... barely able to lift the sheet with the weight of those entries, continues with each page describing more and more horrific accounts of death, the maiming of soldiers, civilians and even the enemy. Death... death everywhere, even death by friendly fire or supposed. A few photos break the tension, but there's something different about them. Could it be they're black-and-white? No, they're color alright! Look closely! Look at their faces! So many have changed... So many new faces... Oh my God... What have they done? Where are the smiles? Where are the cute surfer boys hiding?

Where did they go?

At last, she stops on that page that tells all, the photo of the original pack: shoulder to shoulder, ninety strong... the original rat pack... Joe's Rat Pack...Bravo1, Company B, 2nd Battalion, 3rd Marines. Personal notes, missions, dates, acts of heroism, nicknames, all replaced by End Dates, the faces now hardened by the face of death.

Tears streaming down her face, she realizes this small, war-torn notebook is really an epitaph to the 129 men that Joe swore he would protect. This single spiral notebook bares a weight so heavy, it could sink a soul.

Joe gently lifts the notebook from Annette's lap, reminding her, "It's all right. Today is beautiful and they're at peace in the sun. Come, I'll introduce you to the rest of the gang…

"My Friends on the Wall."

YOUNG MARINES SURFING
CHINA BEACH, VIETNAM
JULY 1967

ONE YEAR AGO TODAY

Four women strong, surrounded in a sea of blue, are here today to honor their fallen brothers. The year has been difficult, the support they share a lifeline to their fragile existence.

When the procession arrives at the cathedral, Blue Uniforms pour onto to the street and down 5th Avenue as far as the eye can see. For this morning marks the first anniversary of the Terror Act of 9/11.

A mayor, his officials, families, friends, a wounded city and a wounded nation stand beside them. At the podium, a bishop prepares to speak to his congregation. With only a faint sound of whimpering and an occasional cry of a child, the cathedral is dead silent...

**One year ago today, our fair city and our loved ones
were savagely attacked by an unknown enemy.
We ask: Why have they been sacrificed?
For what cause could be so great as to steal away the
pure lives created by a loving God?
We ask ourselves, did they die in vain?
Listen...
They want to tell us something as they rest in their
white ivory towers of peace.
Yes, they feel our pain.**

They want us to know they are fine and safe.
They know they were the chosen ones,
The true Heroes, the Martyrs.
While on Earth, they brought
peace and unity to this world.
They are the modest ones, loving and
supporting their families
All they ask is that we share one lesson...
People of the world, tell your leaders in the end, they
will be held accountable to one Almighty Leader.
This Leader doesn't care what you look like,
what language you speak
or your religious beliefs.
He only requires you to be fair and just
in sharing
the gifts he has bestowed on us.
Go and do your business,
be productive, be profitable—
that is all well and good in His eyes.
Only when the Nations of this World
and the Religions they share
come together in Truth
will Peace return to Our Land.

The congregation files out solemnly as the music of the
bagpipes echoes out onto the street. Annette, placing her
fingers in a basin of Holy Water, anoints herself with the
sign of the cross.

The ladies make their way down the crowded steps of the cathedral as camera trucks line the street recording every part of this procession. The outcry of families of the deceased is overpowered by the majesty of this media event. Cameras roll on as they quietly escape, mortally wounded, in search of refuge.

Kissing her sisters, Annette jumps in the rear of a taxi and is greeted by a large, burly eastern man wearing a turban, whom she directs to the East Side to catch her bus.

She reflects on the cost of holy water today.

REFLECTIONS OF
AN ENEMY

Ascending the steps to the Jitney, Annette hands the driver the fare to Montauk, then proceeds down the aisle. Placing her bag in an overhead bin, she takes a window seat, as the bus fills with the many New Yorkers who live and vacation out at the Southeast Fork of Long Island. Resting her eyes still swollen and burning from the tears shed during the day's events, the bus departs 39th Street and 2nd Avenue for Montauk.

After traveling a few blocks, the bus turns into the midtown tunnel. Annette glares out the window, hypnotized by the pattern of tiles that line the walls, each tile creating a memorial to the lives lost in the World Trade disaster. Her trance is broken as the bus exits the tunnel.

Reaching under her seat, Annette retrieves her school notebook from her carry-on and places it on her lap. A host offers a beverage and a snack. She politely refuses. Opening the notebook, she flips through the pages, locating the notes from her first writing assignment in Professor Giannini's class.

Looking out of the window, Annette stares at the cold sight of industrial complexes and cemeteries that line the Long Island Expressway. Turning back, she begins to read her school essay...

Reflections of an Enemy

Two mothers hold their baby boys. Having just been brought into this world, they are free, innocent and happy. They see the world only through the eyes of God. They are pure, living in a beautiful dream of peace and harmony.

As they grow, the world imposes its version of the dream on each child, suffocating the natural beauty given it at birth. The child then rejects itself. Hungry for acceptance, it takes on a value system straight from hell, rich in lies and deception with its sole purpose to blind and control this individual, placing him in line behind the millions of souls that have journeyed this demonic dream.

A mother can only love but can no longer protect her offspring as she hands him over to become part of this illusion called civilization.

In this youth, the child is molded by schools, churches, parents, peers and leaders. What is taught is a distorted, bigoted view of how we as people, children of God, are to share this planet. This lie, this deception, expects and insists on their complete buy in. Their life is manipulated and degraded to a point that one could no longer identify the remains of this once pure being.

This child has become a soldier of war—not their war, but a war by and of this bureaucracy. He is a child trained to kill, ordered to kill, even honored to kill, all in the name of God. This has been the order of man since the beginning of time, yet the dream seems to contradict itself...

"Thou shall not kill."

Our children have now become men confronted on the battlefield, following in the steps of the millions of soldiers who have gone before them.

Annette falls asleep, she dreams.

* * *

The Invasion of Italy

A jeep traveling through a ravine is carrying two Italian soldiers retreating from the heavy artillery of the allies. A young Italian soldier driving his senior officer hits a land mine; the officer dies immediately, his body blown from the overturned jeep. The young soldier, barely conscious, lies in shock next to the jeep bleeding. The sound of close gunfire and voices of the enemy in the near distance arouse his instinct to survive. He makes his way to cover. His face is streaked with blood and covered in soot, his uniform torn bearing the shrapnel that covers his torso. Saved only by the numbing shock that possesses his body, he crawls his way up the grassy knoll to the safety of the tree line.

He dreams of being safe at home with the love of his family and sobs.

Then down on the trail below appears the enemy, a young, lone American soldier. The wounded soldier takes a deep breath as a single clear thought rushes through his confused mind. He considers giving himself up and putting an end to this nightmare.

Studying the approaching soldier, he listens and waits to see this powerful enemy that is overtaking his country. The American now in his sights, the Italian soldier surrenders to war and fires a single round knocking the American off his feet. In a flash, the wounded soldier disappears into the bushy, deep knoll below.

The Italian, stunned by his own action, is not sure if to run in retreat or finish his kill. A remembrance of a once beautiful time hunting with his father in the fields behind their small farmhouse, flashes in his mind. After having shot a deer through the shoulder, a chase ensued to confirm the kill.

Hence he pursues.

The American, bleeding profusely from his shoulder, stands up from the deep grass and clutches his rifle, sensing that he is being hunted by his enemy. Consumed by the will to survive, he inches his way through the tall grass that leads to a grouping of cypress trees where he rests.

The Italian makes his way down the ravine to the road. No longer enjoying the safety of his vantage point, he hunts his prey. Following the trail of blood of the wounded American through the sea of flattened grass leads him to his kill.

The American, now lying in a pool of sweat and blood, waits with his rifle cocked in anticipation of an enemy intending to strike a lethal blow. Beyond fear, beyond pain, running on pure adrenaline, he remains quiet and in the ready.

The Italian, trapped in his mission to kill, thinks back to a time where life was peaceful and beautiful, a life that made sense. He comes to a tree line, now exposed in a small clearing, directly in the sights of the American's rifle. With his finger on the trigger,

The sky goes dark...

The loud echo of a baby's cry
is heard throughout the countryside.

ERVING JOSEPH MARTINEZ
1947
PFC-E3 SCREAMING EAGLES
82ND AIRBORNE

LAST STOP MONTAUK

Annette is startled by a voice. "Last stop Montauk."

Rubbing her face, she collects herself from her deep sleep. With her vision blurred, she remains seated as the last of the passengers file out.

Her surroundings seem different. Overcome with confusion, she suspects she's still dreaming. The bus driver approaches, offering assistance to remove her suitcase. Annette, studying his uniform can't seem to place the odd design as he sets a brown wicker suitcase at her feet. Studying the case, she informs the driver that there must be a mistake because her luggage was new. The driver courteously searches the overhead rack for another bag.

Rubbing her eyes, she stands and scans the interior of the bus. To her amazement, she feels as if part of an old movie. Looking down at the dark brown velour seats, a strange feeling of a time past engulfs her. The bus driver comes back down the aisle and apologizes, stating another passenger may have taken her bag by accident. Turning to him, Annette can't help but notice the metal racks that have replaced the modern overhead bins. Then looking toward the front of the bus, she notices the old change style, reminding her of the buses she rode to school as a child.

The bus driver picks up the suitcase from the floor and sets it on the seat in front of her, exposing a set of monogrammed initials, A.M.O., next to a worn brass latch.

Studying the initials, Annette is stunned. Could they be mine?

Annette Mary O'Gorman

She remains frozen.

The driver, returning to his seat, reaches up to a handle and begins cranking the roll-sign till it reaches the return destination, "Manhattan." A voice inside her mind tells her she is still in her dream and yet her conscious mind says differently. Clutching the wicker suitcase from the seat, she apologizes to the driver for the confusion and exits the bus.

Now standing on the sidewalk as the bus pulls away, she's left choking in a cloud of smoke. Clearing her eyes, she turns to find herself in front of an old, art deco coffee shop, not unlike the many she has seen back home in Brooklyn. Then, from across the street, she hears the sound of screeching tires.

Through the clearing smoke, two old taxicabs are entangled. The drivers engage in an argument as an old black and white police car approaches. Witnessing this picture in front of her, she can't help but realize that she is trapped in her dream.

Turning back to the coffee shop she approaches the entrance, noticing her reflection on the glass door, wearing a dress she has seen before but thinks to herself, "Not something I would wear." Then she glances down at her high-heeled shoes, which resemble a pair she played with as a child before losing her mother.

Amused she enters, walking up to the counter, and takes a seat. Now committed to her new surroundings, she orders a cup of coffee from a waitress in a white uniform and matching cap. Laughing to herself, she muses, "My dreams don't miss a detail."

While she is waiting for her coffee, a gentleman sits next to her at the counter. Placing his newspaper down, he asks for a menu. Glancing over, she sees The New York Tribune bearing the headline "Marines Met with Great Resistance."

In astonishment, she focuses in on the date, September 11, 1942.

Stepping back from this revelation, she counts the number of years to where this dream has placed her from the memorial service she attended this very morning. At that moment, the repeated ringing from the kitchen bell snaps her out of her thoughts. Annette summons up the courage to ask where she could find the East Deck Hotel.

"Well, dear, you're very close," the waitress replies. "All you need to do is walk across the street for a taxi and you'll be there in five minutes."

Feeling relieved, she thanks her, places a dollar bill on the counter and heads to the washroom.

Stepping through the door marked "Madam," she tugs on a string hanging from the ceiling, turning on a single light bulb. Looking straight into the mirror over the sink, she stares at the reflection of a familiar face donning a long-forgotten hairdo. Studying her face, she becomes entranced and overcome by sadness. Tears drop from her big, beautiful brown eyes. Annette is overwhelmed with the feeling her life is slipping away.

Back on the street, she walks across to the taxi stand and asks the driver if he would take her to the East Deck Hotel. The driver smiles, "Why sure, Maam," opening the door. As they pull away, he asks if she has stayed at the East Deck before.

Hesitant, Annette replies, "Why yes, my family has been vacationing here since I was a child."

The driver asks, "Do you remember the damage to the hotel in the '38 hurricane?"

Annette goes silent as she ponders how to answer that question. "We never made it out that year."

"Lucky you, the place flooded when the ocean broke through the dunes. They were closed for six months!"

The taxi turns down a road marked Ditch Plains 1 Mile. They remain silent as they make their way down the bumpy gravel road.

Coming around a bend, a few small bungalows stand engulfed in a sea of tall grass masking the dunes. Ahead, a tall sign marks the arrival to the East Deck Hotel. The driver pulls into the narrow driveway, stops and locks the hammer to the meter. He opens Annette's door, then removes her bags from the trunk. She gives the driver three dollars, which includes a healthy tip. He carries her bags up the wooden steps to the hotel office. Placing them down, he wishes her a good stay, turns and leaves.

At the hotel entrance, the faded white paint and the

distinct smell of mildew mixes with the ocean air to welcome the weary soul to this timeless place of the past. Entering, she rings the bell on top of the check-in desk, summoning the attendant. A women's voice is heard from the back room. "I'll be out in a moment!"

The low volume of a radio station drowning in static plays a contemporary song of the past. Strangely recognizing the room, Annette is mesmerized by the many photos of guests who have enjoyed vacationing at this hotel. She can't help looking for faces of her loved ones.

Suddenly, the attendant appears from behind a white fabric curtain, a matronly looking woman maybe in her seventies, somewhat resembling a distant aunt. She breaks the somber mood with a warm and friendly greeting.

"Hi, I'm Ruth, and you are Annette. Welcome to the East Deck Hotel, we have been expecting you." She then turns the guest register to be signed. "We have you staying until Sunday. Have you stayed with us before?"

Annette is once again perplexed to find an answer. She replies, "This is my first time, but I have always dreamed of staying here."

The attendant chuckles, "Well, that's kind of you, but to dream of staying in a run-down place like this is a new one on me!"

Annette's tension subsides as the ladies laugh. While Annette signs the guest registry, Ruth grabs her suitcase and then leads her down the long wooden deck to her room.

The door opens to a drab, light blue room, exposing a

single bed, a chair and an old wooden dresser with three drawers. Ruth lays her bag on a wooden fold-out valet. Offering Annette a nickel tour of this small space, she leads her into the bathroom and begins pointing out the primitive plumbing fixtures. After a quick look in the single closet, she reminds her that dinner is served promptly at seven. Staring at Annette, Ruth remarks "You so remind me of a great niece I had that lived in New York many years ago. I haven't seen her in ages. She was a beauty just like you. Well, we want you to enjoy your stay, so if there's anything I can do for you, just ask." Ruth closes the door behind her.

Standing in front of the bay window, Annette looks across the vastness of the marsh to the dune that obscures the ocean.

The distant sound of surf is heard through the partially open window, resting her tired soul. She falls into a deep sleep.

A FAREWELL

Friday, September 11, 2002

A cool, clear breezy evening still enjoying the light of late summer...

Guests begin to arrive at the Giannini home, located at Isle of Wight Road in the town of East Hampton, out in the north section known as "The Springs."

An old '80s pickup truck pulls up with its radio blasting, baring a group of grungy looking young men and women. This cigarette-smoking pack approaches across the front lawn. The front door swings open. Vincent appears brilliantly in his Marine Corps Dress Blue Uniform, basking to a standing ovation from this unruly crowd of friends repeating the word "dude" as they critique his new persona. A stark contrast becomes apparent from the Marine standing here today and the childhood buddies he will be leaving behind. The love and devotion they share will transcend a lifetime.

A parade of cars approach fills the driveway and spills out onto the street. Vincent stands point with his parents in greeting the many guests here to honor him today. Down the street, a group of old war veterans, are squaring away their uniforms in preparation for the task ahead. The local surf crowd, always up for a free meal and a party, converges on the hosts as the attention is moved to the backyard. The patio, strewn with its collection of surf memorabilia, offers a wide variety of props for the many long-winded stories of surfing with this hard-core pack. The young short boarders align to taunt the old long boarders with their comical impersonations.

Joe, commander of the barbecue, is engulfed in smoke and flames, flanked by his buddies. Vicky is running mess duty while Alex assumes the position of beverage manager. Mike, the clam man, and Charles, the entertainer, fortify the ranks while Dave smokes a cigarette.

Vicky, preparing a salad, looks out the kitchen window at her son, standing there, handsome and innocent. With tears rolling down her face, she wonders how this could be happening. Her baby is being stripped away, put in the line of fire. She is angry and afraid for his life.

Alone in his room, quiet and removed, Joe Jr., plays a video game shutting out the world.

Vicky and her sister appear from the kitchen with platters of food as Joe announces to the guests, "Let's eat!"

Before the assault on the chow line, the priest stands before them. In silence, they stand to the sign of the cross, followed by the Lord's Prayer and a special blessing for Vincent's safe return. They eat...

The radio plays a slow song from the past as a young lady invites Vincent to dance. He accepts. They engage in soft conversation, sharing an intimate moment, possibly summing up a past romance.

Joe and Vicky watch on from two different ends of the party, divided by the reality of Vincent volunteering to join the Armed Forces and even more, becoming a Marine. The tension between them over war and the commitment to serve this country has driven a stake through the soul of their marriage. Vicky disappears back into the house as Joe and his team lock down the area. The guests have come to enjoy the generous hospitality always given by the Gianinni family over the many years. It is now waning on their marriage.

Vincent cherishes the special attention, knowing he will be isolated from this world for a long time. His mom reappears from the house surprising him with his favorite Carvel ice cream cake. Placing it on the table, she and Joe come together around their son. The cake is inscribed:

Happy Birthday
Lieutenant Vincent Gianinni
Return Home Soon

In one deep breath, Vincent blows out the twenty-one candles, marking his twenty-first birthday as the guests applaud. His mom and dad kiss him on each cheek…

They wonder where this day will lead.

THE ULTIMATE SACRIFICE

Saturday, September 12th

0600 Hours

Joe wakes and heads, downstairs turning on the radio to the local surf report. A hurricane offshore, generating huge ground swells, has been confirmed.

He wakes his sons, sharing a room at the end of the hall. Today will be the last chance for the men to share a surf before Vincent ships out for Iraq. Joe prepares a quick breakfast for the guys, while they lethargically gather themselves.

Suddenly, Joe's cell phone rings—it's George. "I'm down at the Ditch with Alex and Vick. The waves are huge and out of control! Let's get my boat and go to the Block!"

Joe calls to his sons, "Let's go, men, double-time…we're heading to the Block!"

They come down the stairs and each down a bowl of cereal, grabbing their gear as they jump into the old Cherokee and depart for Montauk Marina.

Two hours later, the boat is approaching the southwest corner of Block Island, with its crew of hardcore surfers. The mood on board is upbeat with the usual jokes and surf hype. George maneuvers the boat around the point. The ominous break of the Cell comes into view. The group goes silent. George instructs his crew that they will need to alternate one surfer on board to be designated driver in the event someone gets drunk. The men laugh, breaking the tension.

Vincent volunteers to stand first shift. Placing their surfboards over the side, they paddle out to the break. Joe Jr., not feeling well, excuses himself and stays onboard with his brother.

A nervous mood comes over the men as they paddle in. There are no lightweights here, but the men sense something different today. The waves are heavy, building fifteen to twenty feet with a hard east wind scratching the surfaces into mountainous jagged peaks closing out. George, having navigated this surf before, yells over the ferocious sound of the surf, "Prison Break is going goofy, but will keep you off the rocks. Gas Chambers breaks both ways, and if you wind up in Solitary, you're on your own!" The men deploy.

As they approach, the first set is on them. Vick gets barreled on a short board. Alex, in Gas, takes off on an outside drop, into a triple overhead as Dave paddles away from the group, heading toward Solitary. Joe positions himself in the middle of the ledge between Gas and Prison as a set of four approaches. Suddenly feeling small, as these are the largest swells he's ever been in, he lets three waves go under and paddles into the fourth. Facing his own fear head on, the wave passes over the edge of the rock ledge as he drops down the face. Instinctively jumping to his feet, he turns left down a triple overhead wall, cutting back then left again. The wave is still overhead and beckoning. Having gone one hundred yards, he stalls on the shoulder just a few yards from the boat. His sons yell in approval.

Joe paddles over and relieves Vincent, warning him not to get caught on the inside. Vincent takes his dad's hand and with a gripping hug, kisses him on the cheek, then drops over the side and paddles in.

Vincent paddles over to Gas and settles in, watching a new set approach. Alex and George are about fifty yards to his left doing time in Prison. Vincent drops down the face of a beasty section turning hard right. He's covered up. Joe watches anxiously.

Alex drops on a goofy section while George waits for the next set. Vincent kicks out of his first ride going airborne, proudly waving to his dad. Joe acknowledges, maneuvering the boat to the edge of the break. The attention goes to Dave now isolated deep in Solitary in the face of an outside executioner. Suddenly the trap door collapses under his feet, severing his leash. The executioner masked in spray, from the top of its deep, dark body, traps Dave in its death grip. The men witness this grim task with no sign of life…Dave is drowning in the whitewater of the impact zone.

They pray as crucial seconds pass. Dave's body spasms under the water unable to rise as a second wave buries him even deeper.

Vick struggles to get to Dave with his short board, leaving Vincent closest. Pushing his fear aside, Vincent strokes with all his strength into the Death Zone of Solitary. Joe, alarmed, waits for a chance to move in and rescue his men. Helpless to move closer, he brings the boat around to the north side about fifty yards from Solitary. Dave, breaking the grip of the sea, rises from the foam gasping for air.

Vincent, now just a few yards away, shouts to Dave, "Grab my leash, I'll pull you out!"

Dave grabs the leash as Vincent starts to stroke for the safety of the outside. Then, in a panic, Dave suddenly scrambles up Vincent's back, trying to throw him off his board, tangling Vincent with his own leash. The two attempt to paddle together, making little headway. Dave is smothering Vincent... they're not going to make it through the next set. Vincent removes the leash from his leg.

Vick finally arrives. The first wave collapses, covering the men in a deep soup of foam as Vincent's board spirals into the air. Vincent and Dave are engaged in a fierce battle for survival as another blow of the ax hammers the two in this pugilistic dance with death.

Today the executioner will have his way.

The final blow struck! The life has been drawn from its victim's body. A set of shiny new dog tags sinks to the bottom of the sea, glimmering in the light of death. It now rests in the sand. Vick is there, holding Dave's head above the crashing waves... Dave is rescued!

Joe moves in to pick up his wounded comrades. A voice from the sea...

> "Sir, one Marine is unaccounted for,
> our platoon has lost a son."

WELCOME TO CAMP HERO

Saturday, September 12th

With a knock at the door, Annette awakens. Ruth, the hotel attendant, enters the room with a breakfast tray.

"Good morning, my dear! We missed you at dinner last night. You must be ready for a nice homemade breakfast."

Placing the tray on a small round table in front of the bay window, Ruth draws the curtains, allowing the full morning sunlight to fill the room while she pours a cup of tea.

Quietly, Annette sits up, gazing out through the window.

Staring for a moment at Annette, Ruth remarks, "Do you feel all right? I don't like the color of your complexion."

Annette continues to sit at the edge of the bed in silence. Ruth sits at her side, placing her arm around Annette's shoulder, attempting to comfort her.

"Something has you upset, but whatever it is, it's not worth getting sick over. Would you like to talk about it?"

Trapped in her thoughts and confusion, not wanting to alarm Ruth by exposing her secret dream, Annette breaks her silence. "There was a tragedy in my family. It was a year ago and I'm still struggling with my loss. I just don't understand it, it still weighs heavy on me."

"I'm sorry, Annette. I didn't mean to meddle, but you need to keep your strength up at a time like this if you are to heal."

"You're very kind, Ruth, but I don't think I will ever heal!"

"I understand your pain. It wasn't so long ago my life was upset by loss as well."

"I'm sorry to hear that."

"It took many years to understand my pain, then one day it came to me in an odd sort of way. You wouldn't believe it if I told you."

"What came to you?"

"You might think I'm crazy, but God showed me a sign."

"A sign?"

"Yes, I was walking along the bluff as I had been doing since spring began. I was lost and injured beyond repair. Nothing made sense to me. I did not want to go on. I lost my will to live. I remember it well…the day was sunny but that winter was especially cold and dark, almost unbearable, even for someone strong at heart. The only sound in my empty home was that of music from my radio, reminding me of better days."

Taking a deep breath, Ruth continues, "One day, I found myself walking this trail followed by an odd but beautiful butterfly. I know this sounds crazy and at first I thought I was, but I felt an incredible connection with this tiny insect. I stood there and I watched how it would remain close to me wherever I went, and yet it flew freely from place to place, briefly stopping to pollinate a flower or to sit in the sun on a branch."

"Ruth, my God, that's so amazing!"

Ruth continues, "At first I found it amusing and truly loved the companionship, but as I continued on, I knew I was in the presence of something greater. As the butterfly flew ahead of me, I watched it perch itself on the branch of a blossoming tree. I stopped to take a look; it allowed me to get so close that I was able to see the beautiful design that spanned across its wings. I'm not an expert on butterflies, but I had never seen one with such a unique design. It looked like a great big smile! I didn't move; I didn't want to scare it away. Strangely I felt connected; I had missed being connected to anything since my son's death. He was a soft-spoken young man, quiet, always surrounded by nature. At that moment, the smiley butterfly flew to me and landed on my outreached hand. Annette, I was in shock…at that moment I knew, I was sure! This little butterfly was sent here by God with a message from Ronald, to let me know that he still lives, freer and happier than ever before."

Ruth's face glowing with a bright smile, she goes on, "The butterfly felt glued to my hand, flexing his wings at rest on my limb. My body filled up with life's energy, transfused by this tiny little being. I felt renewed, I felt alive again! I knew I had just been visited by my angel son. You see, Annette, this universe holds many surprises…they don't all make sense, but we must just believe. To believe is to open the door to this universe and allow God to set us free. That day I came to understand that death is not final. I know I may never see my Ronald in this world, but I do look forward to flying with him in the next."

Ruth stands up from Annette's bedside and pulls her to her feet. "Today, you must get dressed and go on an adventure. Get out on the road! Maybe you'll meet your messenger. Every minute of life is precious." With a warm hug and kiss, Ruth leaves the room.

Annette, unsure if she is still captive in her dream, dresses in a pair of shorts, blouse, sneakers and beach hat, and sets out for a walk. Stepping down from the deck in the blinding sunlight, she heads towards the beach.

Along her stroll, her first encounter is the shadow of a large truck piercing through the glare. She stops, reading the sign on the side of the truck: "Ditch Witch," with its menu of specialties. Frozen in time, she remembers buying candy and ice cream from this same truck when she vacationed here as a child.

Walking to the top of the dune, Annette gets her first glimpse of the beach. Today the ocean casts tourmaline-colored waves onto a white sandy beach. Looking to her right, the tall grass-covered dunes extend west for miles. To her left, the dune goes on rising into tall, rocky bluffs with jagged boulders at their feet. Spotting a path, she walks east into the morning sun that soothes her soul. Her journey unsure, her mind unclear, thoughts of a once beautiful life lost, a future with no beginning…

Walking this trail of uncertainty for almost an hour, she is startled by a thunderous sound. Stopping in her tracks, she spots the image of a large airplane approaching the coastline, almost at eye level. The overwhelming vision of an Old World Bomber with its military markings has Annette locked in her dream. As the intruder takes aim, Annette—in a frightening flashback on the World Trade towers of 9/11—is afraid and exposed, stealing her will to go on. In a test of fate, she steps to the edge of this steep bluff. She looks down from the treacherous cliff without fear and prepares to end this dream that has her trapped. She imagines that to fall from this cliff is to live, to become free of whatever has possessed her, maybe to return her to the life she once knew. Annette closes her eyes, begins to fall forward…

At that moment, a voice frantically calls from the sea, "Watch out, watch out, you'll fall, be careful!"

Her date with destiny interrupted, Annette catches herself. Opening her eyes, she follows this voice over the waves and out to sea. She spots the figure of a man mystically standing on water, dancing his way to the sand. She looks on amazed, her eyes following this new addition to her dream.

The young man, staring up at her from below, directs her to walk down the trail that leads to the beach.

Stunned, Annette makes her way down the trail that leads her to a well-built, handsome young man, around six feet tall with thick dark hair and a glistening smile that instantly warms her heart and soul.

"Why, you could've gotten killed getting so close to the edge. Are you okay?"

Annette hesitates. "Yes, I'm fine, thank you. I just seemed to have been walking in a dream."

"Well, Miss…"

"My name is Annette, and yours?"

"I'm Corporal Isabella."

"Well Corporal Isabella, do you have a first name?"

"Yes Ma'am. It's Corporal Robert Isabella." he extends his hand.

"Well Corporal," she replies, shaking his hand. "May I call you Robert?"

"Yes Ma'am."

"How did you manage to get by the MP's that patrol the camp?"

"What camp?" she asks.

"Why Ma'am...excuse me, Annette, you're trespassing on government property. You could be arrested. Didn't you notice the signs? They're all over, like booby traps!"

"No, I'm afraid I didn't. I must have passed right by them. Honestly, I didn't notice anything until that plane startled me."

"Oh, you mean the Navy transport plane."

"I didn't know there was an airport out here."

"Well, there wasn't until recently, but the Navy built a small airstrip to drop off the wounded to Camp Hero."

"Camp Hero, is that what you call this place?"

"Yes! This is the Camp. The men call it kind of a resort outpost for the wounded or just plain damaged. It's a place to heal before going home or getting shipped back to the frontlines."

Annette can't help staring at the young man's body, covered in scar tissue from his waist to his neck. She asks, "Is that why you're here?"

"Yes...as the guys say, I wear my Medal of Honor. Right

now, we need to get you out of here before the MP's arrive or you could be in trouble."

"Oh, I wouldn't want that to happen. I'll find my way back."

"Hold on, I'll show you a secret way out. Follow me."

Picking up his surfboard, he hides it in the weeds, then leads Annette through a maze of large boulders that create the DMZ between the soft sands and the rocky cliffs above. Annette, now in touch with her first combat mission, follows closely behind Robert as he performs his reconnaissance of the trail that lies ahead. He seems different, moving like a jungle cat, invisible, stalking its prey.

They come to a sign. Robert points:

Government Property
DO NOT ENTER
Trespassers Will Be Arrested

Finally, they reach an open stretch of beach, leading them to the lighthouse. Burning through the morning mist, the bright beacon can be seen warning all ships to stay clear.

Approaching this mighty lighthouse with its immense size and strength, their senses are overpowered. The sounds of heavy waves crashing at its base do little to undermine its integrity. Unshaken by history, it stands strong, casting its majestic beam for more than a century, bridging the time between two worlds.

They enter. Looking up at the spiral iron staircase leading to the light, the sound of the sea fills this timeless chamber.

Annette flashes back to her childhood jaunts on the beach, recalling the same sound made from a large seashell she held to her ear, tapping into another world from another time. Asking Robert to lead the way, they begin their ascent. Only moments ago, she risked death to find life and now finds herself playing like a child on a great adventure.

As they come to the first landing, howling winds race through a small open window, filling the lungs of this immense structure. Annette feels secure within, consumed by the power of this mighty relic. She breathes in the cool salt air, invigorating her body, now ready for the final ascent.

The two reach the summit. The eerie hum of the great light echoes as it reigns over the coast, announcing the arrival to our shore. Robert rolls open the heavy iron door to the outer observation deck. A strong wind rushes through. Robert takes Annette's arm, as they fight their way onto the iron grate ledge standing high above the world. Looking out to sea, Annette feels invigorated, infused by a new energy she has long missed. She wonders how this could be happening to her, this dream within a dream. With this great power that has returned, an incredible thought comes to mind. Having reached the end, she has found a new beginning. The two embrace, Annette secure in the arms of this stranger, this new character of her dream.

Stepping outside the lighthouse, the world becomes still. The heat of the day builds with the rising sun. Heading west from the point, they follow the coastline, leaving behind the jagged boulders, delivering them to a magical world by the sea.

The water, at its lowest level, exposes thousands of tidal pools along the shore, glistening in the daylight. These miniature lagoons, sharing their very own eco-systems, separate from one another for only a short while until they reunite with the incoming tide. This mystical world at their feet draws them in ever closer. Our newfound friends share their exploration spawned by a network of oceans since the beginning of time, where for a brief moment in life, man is master. Standing together, gazing into the pool, Annette is blinded by the aura of light surrounding Robert's reflection. She remains still.

Reaching down, Robert traps a tiny crab with his claws extended for battle. Annette watches nervously as the crab maneuvers, snapping at Robert in defense. Robert lets out a scream as the crustacean latches onto his finger and cries to Annette for help.

In her panic, she loses her footing and trips into the pool, only to be saved by Robert pulling her up from the pool into his body. They embrace, looking deep into each other's eyes. Overcome with unexpected emotions, Annette stands before him exposed, helpless in his arms, open to his every move. Suddenly, Robert jumps back, waving his hand in pain trying to break the grip of this tiny predator. In one quick swipe, Annette knocks the beast off Robert's blood-stained hand.

Robert exclaims, "My damsel in distress, my hero!" The two burst out laughing.

The journey continues, Robert leading the way beyond

the tidal pools, traversing a small inlet to a vast tributary enveloped in tall sea grass. The water, only inches deep, gently drains the marsh on its daily journey out to sea. They stop to witness the route of nature's simple mechanism at work; holding hands they enter its womb. The silky sand bottom of the creek caresses their every step, drawing them in deeper. The muddy banks, now lined in fool's gold, are rich with beds of live oysters and clams ready for the picking.

Robert asks Annette if he could borrow her hat. She curiously obliges. Then cutting some reeds of dry sea grass, he quickly weaves a protective lining for the hat. With a quick lesson, she watches Robert smash a large clamshell into a rock, pulling away the broken pieces to expose the raw clam within. He offers it to Annette. To his surprise, Annette takes the shell and in one swoop swallows the clam. Smashing one clam after another, Annette and Robert engage in a primal feast.

Suddenly their adventure is interrupted by the sound of the noonday horn from the camp. Reluctantly, Robert informs Annette he must return for afternoon roll call and will lead her off the camp to the trail where they first met.

Working their way back through the marsh, they follow a small footpath on the west border of the camp delivering them to the bluff. Both sad over this journey's end, they linger on, holding hands as the sound of the surf pounds the shore below, breaking their spell.

Kissing Robert on the cheek, Annette thanks him, walking away from the only person that has freed her soul from that dreadful place of long ago. Robert watches Annette as she makes her way along the trail, then calls to her, "Where are you staying?"

Turning back, she replies, "I'm staying at the East Deck Hotel!" Pointing west, she waves goodbye. Annette now out of sight, Robert turns to the sea and with the sun lighting his face, he smiles.

Robert makes his way through the busy traffic on the base as the barracks empty out before him—a procession of nurses assisting wounded soldiers, making their way on crutches, with broken and missing limbs. He thinks to himself, "And these are the lucky ones."

An ambulance slowly makes its way down Main Street and stops in front of the hospital. The doors swing open; four stretchers are unloaded as the medics attend to the new arrivals.

Further ahead, a caravan of wheelchairs with their attendants creates a gridlock of the most disabled. Robert's appetite passes. His short-lived feeling of tenderness flees his body at the sight of this human devastation. He makes his way through the camp...

He wonders, will they ever heal?

SEARCH AND RESCUE

Saturday, September 12

1100 Hrs

United States Coast Guard Station,

Block Island Sound

Over an emergency broadcast, a distress call is received from a small craft reporting man overboard and a possible drowning off the southeast point of Block Island, commonly known as The Cell. The Coast Guard responds ordering a search and rescue mission, dispatching one MH – 60T, medium-range recovery helicopter and one 187 WPB Response Cutter.

It has been almost twenty minutes since George's distress call reporting a man over board on his VHF radio, with no sign of Vincent. Joe and the men share turns paddling into the powerful epic zone of Solitary that has claimed his son. Refusing to give up, George positions the boat just outside the outer break and cautiously maneuvers.

Relentlessly the sets bear down ever more powerful, forcing the men to stand down and return to the boat. Only Joe remains despite being plummeted over and over...with every set, his buddies are concerned for his life.

Amid the dark sky, an increasing on-shore wind reaching gale force further degrades the surface, endangering the men in their rescue attempt. In a last-ditch effort, Vick defiantly drops his board over the side and rejoins Joe. The two men fight the white water just to stay alive. Finally, the Coast Guard helicopter arrives, hovering overhead. The two men become blinded by its spray and are forced to retreat. The boat repeatedly threatening to capsize, George maneuvers to deeper waters, all praying Vincent's body turns up in the surf.

Almost an hour since the original distress call, the Coast Guard cutter appears from the southeast point of the island, bearing down on the weary men. With a few blasts of its distress horn, the eighty-seven-foot cutter comes to a halt. Sitting on the outside, the cutter lowers a rigid hull inflatable manned by a team of frogmen. The inflatable now underway, intercepts George's boat. Unable to come aboard, the Captain attempts to communicate by VHF only to be drowned out by the sound of the surf.

Joe asks George if he could keep the boat steady when suddenly, without the protection of his surfboard, he jumps into the water and furiously swims to the inflatable. Instantly, the captain of the inflatable issues a Man Over Board distress call over the air, which is intercepted by the helicopter and the mother ship.

Caught in the heavy surf, Joe makes little headway. All eyes are focused. George is unable to bring the boat around in fear of crushing Joe with the hull or even worse, catching him with the propellers backs off.

Fighting to stay on the surface, Joe is being drawn ever nearer to the demon that has claimed his son. Timing his move, the captain of the inflatable throttles his twin engines.

With a burst of white water and foam from a breaking wave, the inflatable reigns down on Joe as a member of the crew casts a rescue hook and quickly whisks him aboard.

Now lying on the deck, choking and spitting up seawater, he points to the location where Vincent was last seen. Sizing up the deteriorating conditions of the impact zone, the captain regretfully informs Joe that he must abandon the rescue mission but the chopper would continue the search.

Dejected, Joe signals to his men to head home,
as he and the inflatable turn back to
the mother ship.

DATE WITH THE HEAVENS

Lying in bed, Annette reflects on her morning's journey, this new amazing character added to her dream...Robert and her close brush with death.

Feeling more comfortable with herself than any time in the recent past, she considers how lucky she was to have been saved by him, avoiding a peril that might have ended her dream or even her life. Something is special about him. Who is he? Why was he there at that moment? Why did she feel safe in his presence?

A knock at the door stirs Annette from this daydream. Expecting Ruth with a reminder about dinner, she opens the door and is surprised to see Robert standing before her with a handful of wild flowers and a beautiful smile.

"I picked these for you." Feeling her emotions bursting, she hugs him. He blushes.

"Well, having met you today, Annette, has brought me luck! Lately, I haven't had much luck fishing, but today that has all changed. I threw a line in and in minutes caught a great big striper!"

"That's wonderful, Robert! You're my man from the sea."

They laugh. Shyly, Robert asks her if she would consider sharing his catch and join him for dinner. Annette is still stuck on Robert's opening words, "Bringing him luck," for it was she who was the lucky one. She accepts.

Robert, elated, offers to pick her up at 7 p.m.

Annette stares in the mirror, brushing her hair, feeling in touch with lost emotions not felt since dating Daniel at college. A smile washes over her face, showering her with the first feelings of joy she thought would never return. Envisioning Robert's beautiful smile, she sees a boy trapped in a man's body with such brave determination to be accountable to his fellow man at any cost. How admirable.

A knock at the door...Robert has arrived!

Despite knowing him for only a brief while, she feels connected to him as if for a lifetime. Stepping outside, she asks if he would wait so she could stop into the office to inform Ruth of her change in plans. Then the two hop aboard Robert's borrowed military vehicle donning two large white stars, one on each door.

Retracing the route used by the taxi, they reach Montauk Highway, heading east following the sign to the lighthouse. Driving only a short distance, they turn left down a dusty gravel road lined with tall pine trees, taking them to the back side of an old rundown marina, where they park.

Leading Annette through an opening in the fence, they climb through. A lineup of old wooden ghost ships, long since sailed now homes to these lost men of the sea, stands silent.

Taking her hand, he leads her to an old houseboat, once a seaworthy vessel for a prominent New York City family escaping the hot summer weekends in the city. Now lying abandoned, this relic offers shelter to this poor soul surviving here at The End.

They arrive at the boat bearing the name Isabella on her

stern and a registration number MTQ444 painted on the side near her bow. Annette feels somewhat amused, as the name Isabella is oddly her mother's namesake.

Robert invites Annette to climb aboard, guiding her as she ascends the transom ladder to the main deck. He exclaims, "Steady as she goes!" They laugh.

Grabbing her hand, he pulls her up to the main deck. Folding down the transom gate behind them, he turns to the cabin door and with a skeleton key unlocks it. Sliding the door open, Robert steps in first, lighting a match and setting flame to the wick of an old brass oil lantern.

He invites Annette in with a bow. Repeating his lamp lighting, he brings the beautifully varnished wood cabin to life with a glow, revealing the beauty of a finely crafted cabinet.

Annette steps inside in awe of this magical environment, studying the character of photographs and books that fill this warm and rich space.

Robert proudly opens a bottle of homemade wine, pouring them both a glass. They toast, "To a day of good luck and good fortune." They strike their glasses.

Enjoying this dream within a dream, Annette can't believe the peace she's long missed has returned ever stronger. She watches Robert as he removes a skillet from a lower cabinet, placing it on top of a small sterno stove. Next he pours some olive oil into the pan and lights the flame. Removing a whole fish from a wooden icebox, he proudly holds up a stealthy black-and-silver-striped demon of the deep. Taking a bayonet from its holder, Robert masterfully fillets his prized catch of the day, a thirty-inch striped bass, and in a few swipes places it onto the sizzling skillet.

Annette opens the cupboard and removes some old plates and utensils, setting the table for their maiden voyage. She boldly suggests Robert open a restaurant when the war is over. He smiles, then enters a dark place in his mind as they dine.

Robert quietly stares out into the darkness, then speaks, "Annette, the world you come from seems to have caused you pain."

Up to now, Annette has been trying her best to keep her two worlds from colliding but to answer honestly she must expose herself and her dream. She looks at Robert, trying to find a way to explain. "In my world, we have enemies too...

"Robert, is there ever a right way to die? Fighting for a belief or falling victim to an unknown enemy. Is there a difference?"

"Annette, I don't really know the answer to that question."

They finish dinner in silence, both hanging on Annette's last words.

Admiring a photograph of Robert in his military uniform, she tells him he reminds her of a movie actor but can't recall which one.

Robert remarks, "Oh, the pretty boy photo."

"Why do you call it that?"

"That photo was taken on my graduation day from boot-camp. The boys call it the pretty boy photo because it's taken before we see combat."

Robert smiles, shaking his head, "That seems like a long time ago. It really wasn't bad, it's just meant to kill the child inside of you…. Anyway, I wanted to fight!"

"So it prepared you for war?"

"War, nothing prepares you for war!"

"That's terrible! What caused your injuries?"

"We were attached to the Fifth Army Division, the first assault wave on the beachhead at Anzio. We were stuck on the beach taking heavy casualties. The enemy artillery was pounding us for more than three days, jamming up the beachhead. Almost all the men in my battalion were killed or wounded. The only protection we had was stacking the bodies of our dead brothers for cover until we were finally saved, what was left of us…by the return of airpower… it was ugly…

"I was knocked out by a mortar round and woke up on a hospital ship heading for the States two weeks later."

"You're lucky to have lived through that!"

"I guess so…but my brothers had to fight on without me." Robert goes silent….. "I belong with them, they count on me."

"Robert, are you saying you would go back there again to face death?"

"Yes…yes, I would. I don't want to be here, cheating life while they die."

"Well, that sounds brave but a bit crazy, if you don't mind my saying."

"That's okay, Annette. It's a code we soldiers live and

die by. I see it would be hard for a civilian to understand."

"It sounds like you're not afraid of dying."

"Standing strong in the line of fire is what we are trained to do. Standing strong in the line of death is a fantasy; we were all scared… every one of us. Death lives with you every moment. It replaces your partner; it digs its way into your soul, clouding your mind. It never takes a day off…it's around every corner, but I'm not afraid anymore. I have a job to do and they count on me. It's not about war anymore or winning—it's about my brothers! I live for them and I'll die for them." A silence permeates the room.

"Robert, I'm sorry I never understood the way a soldier thinks…it's beyond me."

"Annette, it's beyond most who were not there. I trained for this. I thought I was ready, only you can never be ready to see others die."

"But Robert, you've been spared. Don't you see it's a sign you were supposed to live?"

"Annette, a survivor doesn't live, a survivor keeps on dying."

Robert places his head in his hands, collapsing into his lap in despair and cries. Annette covers his head as if to protect him from any more harm. Searching for words of comfort to soothe him through his pain, at that moment she realizes her own despair. Then from deep within, a message is born, something she has been searching for since her own encounter with death.

Rewinding her dream, Annette recalls a lost world left

in chaos, where the victims shared the same commitment to their brothers. The policemen, the firemen, her family, the families of all the victims of 9/11, she wonders how anyone could exist or even die alone without this brotherhood. She never understood this until now. For the first time it all makes sense.

"No, Robert, we live because of them…
that's how we honor them! Don't you see?!"

She clutches his slumped body as if he were a newborn.

Raising his head slowly on Annette's words with tears running down his face, he looks into Annette's glassy eyes. In a soft, almost God-like voice, Robert speaks, "Yes, Annette, we live because of them."

Robert's echo of Annette's own words resonates throughout her being…a message she has been searching for since her tragedy began. An answer, conjured from deep within, a message sent straight from the heavens. She was blinded until now, buried by confusion and self-pity. Rejecting the world she held accountable for her loss, finally she can open her eyes and heart to understand the role of those who survive tragedy. Only then can we begin to heal.

This new message now reverberates deep within, reaching her soul.

"We live to honor them."
Now, the healing begins.

Without saying another word, Robert walks over to the corner of the room and picks up an old accordion lying on the floor. He sits back down and begins to play an old Italian song, filling the room with the sound of a once enemy. Together they sing, stumbling through the lyrics, laughing as God has granted them a reprieve from their torment.

As the curtain comes down to their merrymaking, Robert invites Annette to join him on the front deck for a surprise. Pouring two cups of coffee, they make their way forward to the front deck, where Robert announces with great pride, "The Montauk Planetarium is now open!"

Removing a canvas cover, he exposes an old worn sofa and invites Annette to join him. Together they look up to the sky, tonight brilliantly clear and full of stars on this late-summer moonless evening. Holding hands, they nestle into the sofa. Like a guide to the heavens, Robert points out the many constellations as Annette looks on wide-eyed. The two sit for hours star gazing and mending their souls. When the night chill arrives, Robert covers them with an old army blanket as a shower of meteors puts them to sleep.

Free of their demons,
peace has returned.
All is well.

THE AWAKENING

Early Sunday morning, a cool wind blowing off the ocean whistles through the cabin as the dry, wooden hull creaks. As Annette awakens in her new surroundings, it seems somehow during the night Robert must have carried her into this small sleeping berth inside the forward cabin. She rolls over to see if he is still asleep and discovers his side of the birth empty.

Sitting up, Annette calls out his name…no answer. Where has he gone? Feeling a piece of her missing, she climbs out from the berth, taking two steps up to the main cabin. A pot of coffee awaits her still warm with an empty mug next to a small sugar bowl. "Where is he?" Annette is now alarmed and in touch with deep-seated feelings of abandonment that stem from the childhood loss of her mother.

At the counter, she lights a match, heating the coffee as she reminisces of her conversation with Robert and their beautiful night under the stars. She yearns for his company.

Still dressed from the night before, Annette steps out of the cabin to find a green woolen sweater hanging over the deck rail. Pulling it over her shoulders, she sets out to find him. Climbing down the ladder, she passes the ghost ships, reaching the opening in the fence, turning back one last time to see if he has returned. She resumes her search stepping through the opening.

The car Robert drove is missing. She conjures up a story in her mind that he drove it back to the base and would return for her. Getting her bearings, she walks the same route they took last night hoping to intercept him on his return.

Walking for about twenty minutes with no sign, Annette reaches the highway and waits attentively for him to appear. Remembering the direction of the camp, she plans her route. Heading east on the highway toward the lighthouse, she marches to a steady flow of military vehicles leading the way. With a strong wind directly in her face, she feels even colder and ever more determined. Walking for almost an hour, she spots the entrance to the camp.

Gridlocked in green military vehicles all brandishing white stars, she watches as the guard manually lifts the gate, allowing the traffic through. Her instincts tell her to proceed even further to the east boundary of the camp bordering the lighthouse. There she intercepts the trail she took with Robert on their escape from the bluff. Ahead the seas open up in front of her, the ocean noticeably more violent than she remembered.

The dark sky mixed with a salt-laced wind blinds her vision. Continuing, she ignores the No Trespassing signs and heads for the place she first saw him. Unnerved of being spotted by the MPs, she defies the threat as her quest to find Robert becomes desperate. Every minute the weather intensifies, bringing on gales straight from the far reaches of the ocean as the surf swells up ever larger.

Suddenly, she spots a figure of a man on the horizon

surrounded by mammoth waves. From high on the bluff, she screams to him, reaching out with her arms in a futile attempt to embrace. Robert, trapped in a cage of whitewater, disappears into the lungs of this beast, coughing and spitting in a compulsive display. Something inside her goes dark. Once again, she has been chosen to witness the sentencing of the innocent.

As the ocean erupts, Annette helplessly runs along the edge of the bluff to the trail taking her to the beach below. Trembling knee high in this cold, dark surf, washed by the reach of this violent sea, her body is exhausted. She screams out Robert's name over and over.

> When will he appear and return to me
> performing his magical dance,
> my man of the sea?

From the west, a jeep approaches bearing two MPs. The driver remains in the vehicle as the passenger, a husky Marine sergeant, steps out. "Ma'am, are you okay?"

Annette continues calling out to Robert.

The sergeant, growing concerned, calls to his driver to radio headquarters for backup. Annette stands frozen in the water helplessly drowning in her greatest fear. The sergeant pulls her to the sand. Incoherent she cannot answer him, her limbs shaking violently as the MP wraps her in a blanket.

Crying, she shouts, "He came to me! He saved me. Why did he have to die? Please tell me why! Why?"

At that moment, two more jeeps approach from down the beach and arrive on the scene. One of the MPs opens up a thermos of coffee. Trying to calm her, he pours Annette a cup. The sergeant patiently questions Annette, asking if she could tell him what happened.

Annette, now desperately trying to answer, points out to the sea. "He disappeared…he was surfing and he disappeared!"

The sergeant immediately calls on his radio to headquarters, "We have a potential drowning down here and will need naval assistance, over."

Further interrogating Annette, he asks if she knew the drowned victim. Trying to speak above the sound of the wind and surf, she shouts, "His name is Robert Isabella. He's a wounded soldier."

The sergeant gets back on the radio and requests his records. He then deploys his men across the beach and up on the bluff in search of the lost man.

His radio rings back from headquarters. "Are you sure?"

"Isabella, that's right."

"No record."

"What do you mean? Alright, check it again; I need Navy Frog men down here on the double, over!"

The sergeant hangs up and approaches Annette.

"Okay, ma'am, one more time…your soldier friend, his name is…?"

Annette, shivering, answers again.

"Isabella, Corporal Robert Isabella."

"Now, tell me one more time slowly, what happened to him?"

"He was out there," Annette points, "way out there on his surfboard when a large wave hit him, then he disappeared."

The sergeant interrupts. "Hold on, a what, on a what? Ma'am did I hear you correctly? Did you say a surfboard?"

"Yes, a surfboard."

Perplexed by her answer the sergeant inquires, "What's a surfboard?"

Before Annette could answer, a ring sounds on the walkie talkie. The corporal answers, handing it to the sergeant, "Go ahead, this is Sergeant Davis, over."

He listens, shaking his head side to side. "Well, you're sure of that, no such name listed? Let's notify the town police, this is a civilian matter. We have her down here on the beach…yes, that's correct, no signs yet of a missing man, over and out."

The sergeant confers with his men. Believing Annette may have been mistaken or even undergone a psychological trauma, he orders them to continue the search. Turning to Annette, he attempts to console her until the police arrive. Softly speaking through the clamor of the sea, he assures her his men will do their best to locate her friend but informs her she will need to vacate the base. Annette nods in agreement.

Minutes later, two policemen are escorted by the MPs down the trail leading from the bluff and head directly to Annette. Holding herself together once again, helpless in this dream, feeling scared and alone, she welcomes their protection. Conferring with the Sergeant, the police escort Annette topside to their car and report into headquarters. The police car slowly makes its way through the camp. Annette is enthralled by the vision of wounded soldiers that surround them as they drive through.

The officer asks, "Where are you staying?"

Annette replies, "At the East Deck Hotel," as they pass the guard house exiting the camp.

Still in a state of shock, Annette thinks of Robert. What has happened to him? Was that really him in the water? Then a staggering thought intrudes…

"Was he real or was this another trick
played on me by this dream?"

As the police car arrives at the hotel, the door to the office swings open. As Ruth approaches, the policemen question her. "Ma'am do you know this lady?"

Looking through the back window at Annette staring straight ahead, Ruth answers the officer. "Why, yes, she's a guest here. What happened to her?"

One of the policemen informs Ruth that the MPs at Camp Hero found her standing in the water alone and in distress; she seemed to be upset over the loss of a friend, a drowned soldier. Ruth tells them it seems odd, since she has barely left her room. The policeman opens the rear door, helping Annette to her feet.

"Ma'am, before we hand her over to you, we recommend you call a physician to make sure she's alright."

Ruth takes her hand. "I'll do just that. Now, I'll take her to her room, if you don't mind." Taking Annette by her arm, she leads her to her room.

"My dear, you're still shivering, your hands are ice cold, you could get pneumonia...I'll call a doctor." Helping her into bed under the warmth of the covers, Ruth informs Annette to rest until she returns with the doctor. She agrees.

Looking at the walls and ceiling of this old hotel room, Annette wonders if in fact her mind has slipped away and has been brought to a home for the impaired. Could it be I've lost contact with reality? Will I ever get it back? Or will I be lost in this world of imagination forever?

Suddenly she hears voices, the door opens. It's Ruth and the doctor.

Sliding the single wooden chair over to the bed, this kind old man greets Annette. Gently taking her hand in his, he softly asks how she is feeling.

Fearful of giving the wrong answer, she tells the doctor she's been having bad dreams and hasn't slept well. He listens. Then from his black leather bag, he pulls out a thermometer while he speaks to her. "You seem to have been exposed to the cold."

Annette informs him she got lost on a walk down on the bluffs. Shaking the thermometer, he places it in Annette's mouth as he quietly consults with Ruth.

Returning to her bedside, he examines her, then checks her temperature. He remains silent. Holding her hands softly for a moment, he shares his conclusion.

"My dear, you're running a fever and you seemed to have been traumatized. Sometimes we shut things out and they remain inside until we deal with them. Have you experienced something of this nature?"

Annette stares blankly.

"I am going to give you a light sedative to help you rest. Tomorrow, Ruth will serve you a good meal to help you regain your strength. I further advise when you return home you seek the help of a qualified physician to help you sort out whatever it is that's troubling you." Taking out a hypodermic needle from his case and a small ampoule, he withdraws the sedative and injects Annette.

Ruth stays by her side as the doctor leaves.

Annette sleeps.

SOLITARY

Sunday, September 13th

Sitting at the table in the Block Island Coast Guard Station, Joe, having just hung up the phone with Vicky, quietly tries to understand.

"How could this have happened?"

An officer pours a mug of hot coffee and sets it in front of him. Shivering, he places his cold weathered hands around the cup, absorbing its soothing heat. He sits distraught with emotion. His concern over Vicky's well-being weighs heavy on his mind. She is expected to land at the airstrip within the hour. He wonders how he will be able to face her.

A soldier, a surfer, a death wish,
all the same in her eyes!

"Am I responsible for this?"

A Jeep is dispatched, taking him to the airstrip. A single-engine craft lands and taxis to the small terminal building at the north end of the runway. Joe runs onto the field, anxiously waiting for Vicky to exit. The door opens and the two embrace. Carrying her bags to a taxi parked outside the terminal, they sit silent for the five-mile drive to the Solitary

Inn. The inn is located at the southeast corner of the island, only hundreds of yards from where their son was last spotted.

Arriving, Joe pays the driver as Vicky climbs the white wooden staircase of this two-story Victorian home perched on the rocky cliffs. Reaching the front door, he turns the heavy brass knob, swinging it open against the howling winds. He turns to find Vicky stiffly staring into the dark, listening to the violent sound of the sea crashing on the rocky beach below. The cold chill of the air fills their bodies with the stark realization of their loss. They enter.

The following morning, Joe and Vicky sit quietly in the dining room, alone and apart. Staring out the large glass picture window giving them a full panoramic view of the sea churning as if a violent death machine, they pray for Vincent to appear.

The surf pounds the rocks below, crushing them into pieces just as it did the life of their son. Looking deeply into each other's eyes, they join hands across the table.

Their minds travel back to a distant place and time through the caverns of life to a place of joy and happiness, to the time of creation where the first seed was sown. Vicky murmurs, "Where's my baby?"

Joe sits stunned, immobile, shells exploding all around, dug deep into his trench, desperately trying to stay alive and protect his men. He can't lose Vicky. He musters all his strength; he would sacrifice his life to save her. The burden of life and death has once again been placed on his shoulders.

The delicate silence is broken by the sound of the wind

as it rushes through the open door of the inn. The desk bell rings, summoning the attendant. Muffled voices are heard as footsteps head in their direction. The hostess cautiously interrupts, "I'm sorry, folks, but these gentlemen are here to see you."

The dining room starts to spin as the sentence of death comes down on this family. "Excuse me, I am Captain McGuire and this is Second Lieutenant Ogden."

With a consoling face, he pauses.

Desperately Joe and Vicky pray that they snap out of this nightmare, listening as the officer continues.

"This morning at 0600 hours, our rescue party retrieved your son...on the southeast coast of the island about a hundred yards from where he was last seen."

The lieutenant interjects, "We were lucky to find him so soon."

The couple sits motionless, unable to make sense of the officer's remark. The Captain announces, "We have his body at the base infirmary and would like you to join us to identify your son. As Vicky stares out the window void of emotion, Joe asks them if they would wait out front while they go to their room to get ready.

The officers head out of the dining room. Standing up from the table, Joe holds Vicky's arm and escorts her to their second-floor room. Opening the door, Vicky heads for the bathroom, locking herself inside. Joe stands numbed by the sound of Vicky's outcry cutting through his heart and soul like a jagged knife.

Once again a witness to death, Joe is unable to deal with his own grief, his pain bottled up inside.

They arrive at the Coast Guard Base and are met by a Naval doctor and his staff of two escorting them to the infirmary. A set of large doors swings open to a white cavernous room, exposing a lone, stainless-steel gurney draped with a white sheet.

The moment of reckoning bears down on these poor, loving souls. As the sheet is pulled back, Vicky turns away, her body postured, stiff and erect, wrapped in her husband's arms. Joe stares down, nodding in acknowledgment.

"Yes, that's our son."

Joe…suffocating from this medal of guilt,
this medal of failure,
hung on a man of honor.

MORNING AFTER

Annette is sound asleep, safe in a world of silence filled with rich colors, free of all thoughts in a place close to heaven, her soul floating among the clouds in touch with the spiritual world.

How can a God so kind and merciful make such
demands on one's soul?

A God who welcomes you to share His beautiful
creations, then with one quick blow strips them away.

Or could this be the work of another agent known for his
crafty work of deception?

One will never know why we are tested.
It's just a fact of life.

Yet, here Annette sleeps, ever peaceful, ever alive, close to the end of her journey.

Ruth draws the curtains, ushering in a new act called today.

Annette awakens from her sleep to the sunlight of the new day. Opening her eyes, she is embraced by the sweet sound of her guardian Ruth.

"Good morning my dear, did you sleep well? Would you like some tea?"

Ruth turns on the radio to a station playing familiar music. Annette's eyes dart around the room, her senses quickened. Something's different, could she be back in touch with the world she left?

Realizing today is today,
her dream has come to an end,
she smiles.

Her energy is revitalized, her complexion has returned. Standing up, she hugs Ruth as the two women dance to the beat of a new day. Feeling free, she opens the closet door, holds up a colorful dress to her body and announces: "Today I will take a walk and find the answer to my dream."

Ruth, encouraging Annette to embrace every remaining minute of her stay, reminds her she has confirmed the bus reservation for 5 p.m. on the jitney returning to the city. Secure in Annette's well-being, Ruth kisses her on the cheek and returns to her duties. Annette, now dressed, heads out on her new day's journey. Memories of Robert, still daunting, lay heavy on her mind. How could a man so beautiful, so real, not be real? She decides to take it slow. After a year of torment, she need not bury herself again.

Taking a different route to a once familiar place, she journeys toward the lighthouse. Today the streets are lined with small, brightly painted wooden cottages. Annette can't help but notice the many surfboards that adorn this landscape. Thoughts of Robert as he walked on the water coming from heaven to rescue her are still clear in her mind. She finds herself stepping onto Montauk Highway, just a short distance to the road that will take her to the old marina. "How could this be?" she asks herself. "Will I ever free myself from this dream?" Letting her will take control, she turns down the dirt-covered lane compelled to find the answer.

Engaged in this psychic game of chance, Annette wonders what she'll find when reaching the old marina. The woods that line the road show no telltale signs. Nearing the end of the lane, her eyes are drawn to the opening in the chain link fence. As she approaches the corner, the marina comes into full view.

"Be careful what you wish for," she thinks to herself.

Just as she remembered, a line of old abandoned boats lay across the landscape as did the ghosts of '42. Walking up to the old, still rusty fence, she spots a young man working on a surfboard. Her day's journey now turns a new corner, remembering the magical night under the stars in the arms of Robert, fondly thinking "my man of the sea." Even more intent on making sense of this loss, once again summoning the courage to test fate, she searches for the ship "Isabella."

"Excuse me, sir, would you know where I might find Robert? He lives aboard the Isabella."

The young surfer, holding a sanding block and covered in white dust, turns to Annette, raising his head in an attempt to pull the name from the heavens. He draws a blank. "I'm sorry lady, I've only been here three months… there's no one here that I know with that name. Are you sure he's in this boatyard?"

"That's okay, I'm not sure," she frowns. "Maybe I'm in the wrong place."

In light of her disappointment, Annette's quest to find Robert gains momentum. She heads for the beach. Returning down the lane, she scours the woods for any sign that would catch her memory, but it's just a blur. Breaking a sweat in the noonday sun she reaches the highway.

Without hesitation Annette turns left, heading east towards the lighthouse. Recounting her last trip here, she is interrupted by a new model sports car with a powerful sound system.

Taming her imagination, she thinks, "At least the traffic today is not all drab green."

Each car that passes fills the spectrum of the rainbow, when out of the corner of her eye, she spots an eerie sight. Protruding from the overgrowth that has reclaimed this past sanctuary is the sign "Camp Hero." Today there's a guardhouse, but no guard, no lineup of vehicles waiting to service the camp and the wounded souls within. There are no signs to ward off trespassers. She enters. Walking down the rutted road, she finds herself flanked by pillboxes and foundations of a once thriving community. No signs of the many damaged people. Where did they go? How could she have lain witness to this ghost ship of souls? She stops in the center of town where the hospital once stood, now only bearing traces of a stone foundation. Across the road, the chapel where the poor souls lined up for the noonday mass begging God's refuge, has now disappeared.

"I've been here. How else could my mind draw such a complete picture? Where is Robert? If this is real, then he was real…"

She walks further down the pitched road that leads to the bluff. Most of the town has been reclaimed by nature, along with many of its inhabitants. Yet, standing tall, defying the test of time, a radar tower still stands, ready to warn us if friend or foe.

How is it that some things are more resilient than others, able to ride out the storm and still keep their shiny armor? Annette reaches the bluff. Now evermore determined to find Robert, she looks to the sea. Why would I be here if the dream were not true? Why won't it let me in?

Today the sea is calm. The dark skies are emboldened with ominous clouds, but no sign of Robert. Following the trail that leads to the beach, she wonders, maybe he's here among the rocks waiting for me to appear. Oblivious to the dangers, she makes her way down the steep passage with its loose jagged rocks, anticipating a reunion.

Finally reaching the soft white sand, not how she remembered it, she searches ever desperately.

Her dream is near.

On the beach, she journeys toward the spot where he first came to her from the sea. She begins to cry, desperately waiting for Robert to appear. Looking to the sky, she drops to her knees, "I know he's here…"

Digging her hands deeply into the sand, she reaches to the heavens, imploring God to show her a sign. A strong wind gusts off the ocean and rushes through her body filling her with the energy of a pure spirit!

The sand runs through her raised hands as a sharp ray of sun breaks through the dark clouds, lighting a rusty silver chain resting between her fingers, exposing a set of old dog tags. Wiping her eyes, she looks closely at the rusty half-missing tag, revealing the last four letters of a name, 'e-l-l-a' and the last part of a serial number 0444.

From her hands, the rays of the sun travel out to sea, lighting the cradle resting Robert's soul.

God has let her in.

A FALLEN HERO

Monday, September 14th

After a short twenty-minute flight, the Giannini family arrives at East Hampton Airport. Stepping down from the small private plane, they are greeted by their close neighbor, Ron, and their son, Joe Jr.

Vicky embraces Joe Jr. and walks to the car, leaving Joe to carry their luggage. Their son quietly walks by his mom's side, holding her arm tightly, confused and fighting his tears. Ron grabs a small suitcase and runs to open the car door as Vicky helps Jr. into the back seat. They drive home in silence, Joe's desire to emotionally comfort Vicky, rejected, as she sits coldly removed.

Reaching the house, they are met by a sea of reporters blocking the entrance to the driveway, snapping photos of the family as the car makes its way through. Stepping out from the car first, Joe shields Vicky and his son from the fervent press attack. One reporter of a local paper intrudes, "Sir, is it true that your son was drinking beer just before the time of the accident?"

Another reporter asks, "When was he to leave for Iraq?"

They make their way to the front door as the neighbors look on from their front yards. Inside the house, Joe drops the bags as Vicky heads to the kitchen. Drawn to the window where she last saw Vincent standing tall and proud...

147

Her boy, pretending to be a man,
wearing a uniform of deception.

Suddenly Vicky's anger rages.

"You stole my son, you...
you took him from me!"

Joe rushes to her side,
only to be pushed away.

Helplessly, Vicky looks out the window
onto the farewell party of her child.

MONTAUK TO MANHATTAN

Monday, 5 p.m.

A radio is blaring pop music as Annette tidies herself for the trip home. A huge weight has been lifted from her shoulders, yet she doesn't feel free. The thought of returning to her world is clouded by the realities of her great loss and chronic loneliness. Still, she is obsessed with finding the meaning of her dream: Robert, Camp Hero, her new friend Ruth. Yet somehow she finds solace in recollection of all the characters that came together on this remarkable journey.

How could she have felt this healing if it weren't for meeting Robert and Ruth, her first maternal connection since the loss of her mother many years ago. Why, if it weren't for this dream, her life—or what was left of it—was doomed to despair. Today she has returned to herself, a bit damaged, but again she is Annette.

A car horn honks outside the hotel...it's Ruth. Annette grabs her bag, taking one last look around this simple room that sheltered her through this emotional storm. Opening the door, she is met by a fragrant breeze from across the marsh. The sun is beginning to set and the sound of the sea can be heard softly caressing the beach. The full breath of life has returned to her, her senses fully restored. Ruth is parked in front of the hotel office in a shiny, red 1958 Cadillac convertible with its top down. She calls to Annette. Approaching from down the deck that adjoins the rooms,

Annette is sporting a shiny, new Louis Vuitton valise. Placing it in the rear seat, together they head down the lane leading to the highway. Ruth is wearing an old flowered silk scarf tied over her head, while Annette's hair blows freely. The two friends chatter incessantly all the way to town.

Arriving on Main Street, Ruth maneuvers a wide U-turn in the middle of the block, rolling up to the bus stop. Annette catches herself looking for the old taxi station across the street, now inhabited by a car service, bearing a phone number of all 4's. She smiles, wondering, "Where have I seen those numbers?"

Ruth removes Annette's bag and places it on the sidewalk. Looking at each other lovingly as if having lost a lifetime apart, Annette thanks Ruth for her kindness.

Ruth, holding Annette, laughs with tears streaming down her face. Never having a daughter of her own, she now feels blessed, asking her to promise to visit again soon.

The women embrace as the bus pulls up. Having bonded their souls, the two ladies savor every last drop of this newly found family.

The electronic roll sign displays its destination, Manhattan.

Annette boards.

DRESS OF HONOR

Tuesday, September 15
New York City
Joe and Vicky arrive at the chapel on the Upper West Side of Manhattan, only a short distance from the family's house of worship, Saint Bartholomew Cathedral.

Inside the chapel lies the body of a lost Marine, a hero, a son, United States Marine Corps Lieutenant Vincent Robert Giannini.

Life has dealt our family a deep blow!

Loving parents dedicate their lives for the betterment of their offspring, clearing the way, so they may find fewer obstacles on their path through life.

Why are children taken from their parents
at such a young age?

It isn't fair…it isn't natural.
It's against everything we believe in,
but it happens.

Today our son, our beautiful son, lies in front of us dressed in the uniform of a man, a soldier. How did this happen? When did this happen? We never looked away…"

151

Vincent's body is lying there, handsome in his Marine Corps Dress Blue Uniform. Looking like a fine escort to a gala event or an attaché to the President, he now lies motionless, void of expression, unable to share his point of view. His identity stolen before having a chance to leave his mark on the world, a precious flower lost in bloom.

Reflection

We are all inhabitants of this planet. We value our lives, but do we value our creation? We are fractioned, tribes if you will, removed from each other over and over by this plan called civilization. A plan designed to manipulate and steal our instincts to share life's bounty. To rise above the weak and conquer our neighbors, stealing their gifts for our own gain...

Is war not the ultimate sin, a sin committed every day by the great nations of this planet? How sad. At least if there is one consolation to this horrible tragedy, I truly believe God, the Ultimate Power, the Giver of Life, has a beautiful answer for us. Yes, I do believe there is a paradise, a soft totally silent resting place for the soul to bathe in the light of the stars. A dimension just around the next corner, the best of us reach this place first; be patient... you'll make it."

His father places a set of shiny new dog tags within his hands, covered with pure white gloves...

My Beautiful Boy in your Dress Blues

444 – THE MESSENGER

Annette returns to night school, now healed from the wounds she carried so deeply before meeting Robert. Who was he and how did he come into her life, a character from a dream, yet so real?

Taking a seat near a window, she stares out to the still lit sky. Removing her notebook, she searches for the page "Reflections of an Enemy." Her project notes incomplete, replaced by the dream, leave her confused and wondering how to tell the story that delivered her to another world in another time. How do I share this dream that took my life to the brink of disaster, or do I just tell of the healing that eventually touches those souls who value life in honoring death?

The classroom clock shows 6:10 p.m. with no signs of Professor Giannini. Annette feels the deep connection she experienced on the field trip that took them to the Vietnam Memorial and how he reminded her of her dad. Warm, kind, gentle men, veterans of war…how could they be capable of hurting someone, or even killing? She dismisses the thought. Her dad respected the men that served in that war, kind of like old teammates from a bygone season. Dad really kept his pain hidden deep down inside. At night time, those demons would awake, erupting from his chest like an alien force. I remember the cries…how did he live with such pain?

The other students file in and begin reviewing their reports, while others engage in light discussion. The classroom door opens. A young man, looking more like a student, carrying a brown leather briefcase, walks up to the desk.

"I'm Professor David Goldstein. I'll be filling in for Professor Giannini. He unfortunately had a death in his family and will be out for an undetermined amount of time."

The students, taken back by this sudden news, sit quietly. Annette, once again sensing loss, is touched by this news. The professor asks the class to bring him up to date. Understanding the initial writing assignment, he asks for a volunteer to share their work.

A young woman raises her hand and begins to read a well-thought-out essay. The class listens attentively to her views on innocent civilians, casualties of war, and the abuse of military might in reaching their objectives. Members of the class become aroused by her personal insights attacking our government in its quest for oil domination, setting off a heated discussion. The professor, gloating in the light of debate, further stirs this potential mob with his own leftist views.

Forty minutes later and only two essays read, Annette remains silent. Unable to join in the same old political rhetoric that has cost so many millions their lives, she thinks to herself, this is not what I signed on for. A thought crosses her mind...who died in Mr. Giannini's family?

The bell sounds the end of class. Students file out in heavy debate. Annette approaches the professor, still in intensive discussion imposing his point of view. She waits patiently.

Finally turning to Annette, he hastily closes his briefcase and begins heading towards the door.

"Excuse me, Professor, what do you know of Mr. Giannini's loss?"

"Sorry, I didn't get your name?"

"Annette O'Gorman."

"Well, Ms. O'Gorman, I was called in at the last minute to fill in and I really wasn't privy to the news, but I believe it had something to do with a drowning. If you're concerned, why don't you just Google it in the library?"

The professor disappears down the hall, leaving Annette locked in on the "drowning" word. She marches across the street to the university library and patiently waits for an open computer. She Googles "Giannini Family Death." A déjà vu of the screens of death in Times Square on the morning of 9/11 come into view, now depicting:

A MARINE HERO...

dies saving a fellow surfer during a coastal storm. Marine Corps Officer Graduate, Vincent Robert Giannini, the son of a prominent New York defense attorney, drowns off the coast of Block Island, while trying to save a fellow surfer.

Scanning further down the article, she sees the name and address of the chapel in bold. Noting the last service taking place this evening at 7:30, her watch shows 8 p.m.

Annette's senses now tap into her dream.

She quickly copies the address and heads to the street for a taxi.

Arriving at the chapel with only minutes before the end of the final service, she squeezes through the large crowd gathered on the sidewalk. Annette, once again captive in her crusade to find the answer to this dream, makes her way inside.

A strong outpouring of emotion resonates throughout the chapel as the line moves slowly toward its resting place. Standing along the wall, a group of young men are huddled, engaged in animated conversation, recalling the many wild episodes shared with the deceased. A row of young women sits teary-eyed, supporting one another as they mourn the loss of a dear friend.

At the head of the chapel, Annette spots Joe standing next to a priest, surrounded by grievers offering their condolences to the family. Deep in her mind still puzzled by her dream, she puts the pieces together: the loss of her family, 9/11, her story "Reflections of an Enemy," Robert and now the loss of Joe's son—somehow it all ties together.

Reaching into her purse, she removes the set of rusty dog tags, her only connection to Robert. Holding them, she prays.

Finally arriving at the foot of the casket, Vincent's body is hidden from view, masked by mourners. Annette stares down at a pair of black patent leather shoes partially covered by blue trousers trimmed with wide red stripes running up the seams. Her anticipation to finally meet Vincent rises.

The clock speeds ever faster
as time remains frozen.
The answer is near.

Recognizing Annette, Joe walks over to her and extends his hands. She covers them with both of hers, kissing him gently on the cheek. He thanks her for the kind visit. As the kneeler empties, Annette takes a step forward.

A numbing feeling takes over her being. Tuning out the world, she returns to a special place. A place of refuge for the broken of will. A place of salvation. She kneels. Face to face before her lies the answer to her dream.

Feeling the presence of something familiar, she stares at Vincent. I know him…I feel his soul drawing me in. He bears a striking resemblance to Robert.

Placing her hands on Vincent's ignites an energy inside her unfelt since Robert held her close that magical night under the stars.

Remembering the butterfly that came to Ruth from her son, she feels ever closer to her messenger.

Her primal instinct to cry is answered as Joe places his hands on her shoulder.

Vicky, sensing Annette's special connection with her son, walks over and kneels down beside her.

The chapel turns silent. The roses that drape across the back of the casket seem to link the souls of all the departed. A set of shiny new dog tags, glistening in front of her, hold the answer.

Annette takes Robert's rusty dog tags,
holding them up for all to see.

The host of God's beautiful work,
this masterpiece,
a visit from an angel
sent from the sea...

The serial numbers ending in:

444

matching those of Vincent's.

Annette, surrounded in the safe harbor of Vincent's aura, places the old rusty dog tags in Vicky's hands.

"These are for you. I now understand why they came into my life. Vincent was my angel."

The priest turns to the congregation, and with the sign of the cross begins to pray:

Psalm 444
"God's Messenger"

Believe in the Lord
as sheep follow their shepherd
through the dark pastures.

The Lord is the light,
and the life.

His angels,
the shepherds protect
his children from
pain and suffering.
Believe in the Lord
and you will be set free.

Annette has found her angel.
A beautiful soul lives on,
her dream fulfilled.

THE HEALING BEGINS ...

THE END

**A wave sent from the Heavens
to reclaim one of God's greatest gifts,
"My Son"**

YOU ARE ABOUT TO ENTER THE

CAMP HERO

FOOT LOCKER

BEWARE:
STRONG SOULS
RESIDE WITHIN

**Decorated United States Marine Corps Captain
Joseph A. Giannini, Esquire
1967
First Battalion Third Marines, a.k.a.
The Home of the Brave**

THE REAL-LIFE CHARACTER JOSEPH GIANNINI, ESQ.

Today Joe and his wife of twenty-seven years still live in the quaint beach community of the Springs in the Town of East Hampton, New York.

The Gianninis are a loving and dedicated family still challenged by life's call.

Joe, at the age of sixty-eight, struggles with PTSD (Post Traumatic Stress Disorder) and the early stages of the disease caused by Agent Orange, a toxic pesticide ground killer used to clear foliage during the Vietnam War.

Joe has had his own Saturday morning Veterans cable TV show airing in Long Island, New York, and remains on the front lines as an anti-war activist. He has published a number of stories, journals and newspaper articles throughout the northeast region. He travels around the United States supporting his beliefs and consoling his many damaged brothers from wars past and present.

He is a kind, gentle man and can still be found in the lineup, surfing out in Montauk. Just look to the outside where the big waves live and you'll spot him waiting for the clean-up set.

He is working hard every day to keep his law practice alive and would love to have your business. So, as Fred Gwynne said in the movie *My Cousin Vinny*:

"He's one hell of a lawyer and one hell of a HERO."

ACKNOWLEDGMENT TO THE LIFE AND WORKS OF JOSEPH GIANNINI

I want to thank Joe for his friendship and opening up his life stories in creating *Camp Hero*. We spent much time together over the years surfing out in Montauk and sharing stories about life and the Vietnam War.

As a Veteran Marine and surfer, I've come to appreciate the strong Brotherhood that bonds us together and the shining example of a true hero.

Joe is passionate about spreading awareness of the damages of war. He has allowed me to use a number of his published works in developing this story. These true accounts and memoirs have provided inspiring insight for the fabric of *Camp Hero*.

ABOUT THE CHARACTER ANNETTE O'GORMAN

Our character is based on a cross-section of the many survivors of 9/11 who suffered the loss of loved ones on that tragic day. Although she is not an actual person, her character was created to convey the emotional trauma felt by all who lived and continue to live through this tragic experience.

The journey taken by our character to reach a place of healing was part drawn from our own personal experience, having also lost a son that fateful year of 2001.

Although nothing in this world will ever bring him back into our lives as the beautiful young man he was, we find comfort in a spiritual connection, as portrayed in this story.

It is through Annette's character we express the great pain incurred from this terrible event and the eventual answer that begins the healing.

We hope this story has reached your heart
and helps to heal your soul.

WAR GAMES

War can
shatter the child.
War can
shatter the man.
But War can
never shatter the child
in the man.
Surfing defies this.

CFC 333

ACKNOLWLEDGMENT

Our undying gratitude to our West Coast Brothers for their amazing book and DVD,

"Between the Lines"

This true account of the California surf culture, through a time of war and politics during the Vietnam War, has inspired so many of us to understand the true complexities of the Vietnam War.

Jerry Anderson, Publisher
Scott Bass, Producer/Director
Ty Ponder, Director
Troy Page, Director of Photography, Editor

Thanks, to Greg Samp and the many fine Veterans and members who contributed so generously to make that story possible, along with the photography displayed in this book.

Special thanks to the Brotherhood of surfers and Veterans who have carried on this rich tradition.

VIETNAM VETERANS MEMORIAL PADDLE-OUT

Oceanside Pier & Amphitheater
September 30, 2007
Oceanside, California

Our sincerest thanks to
Jerry Anderson, Event Chair,
and his devoted wife, Debbie

www.BetweenTheLinesFilm.com
www.HeadlineGraphics.com

CALIFORNIA DREAMING

My tour in Vietnam was an incredible evolutionary delusion,
one I think shared by many. The delusion you ask:

War for Peace

The insane ego-driven spiral of perpetration and retribution,
action and reaction, all in the name of freedom:

Yet in the middle of it all was
Love

Much has been recorded regarding the politics, the violence
and the heroism of the time, but for a small group of
surfers it was a time of personal growth. A time for us
to do and share with others what we loved deeply:
riding waves.

It is hard to believe that in the midst of a war there was
a "Safe Zone" where soldiers and civilians were temporarily
pardoned:

China Beach, Vietnam

Although only a mere flash in the picture of war and
devastation, it was enough to keep us from becoming
unglued.

I yearn to get back to the earth, to the sea, to the things
that I knew were real and true, I need
to come back home, to my
California Dream.

Tom Woods
Sea Wolves, U.S. Navy, Vung Tau

A SURFER IS WHO I AM

Gentlemen:

Although we didn't serve together, it felt like we did. Being a Vet is a special part of my life.

Being a surfer is who I am and what I'll always be.

Finding all of you, who shared these experiences, man that's magical!

The paddle-out itself, a time to honor our brothers who didn't make it back to the world.

We won't forget them.
"God Bless and Semper Fi"

Ralph Fatello
U.S.M.C., Vietnam Veteran
Vietnam Veterans Memorial Paddle-Out
September 30, 2007
Oceanside, California

THE INVISIBLE HERO

I feel like we have gone full circle within ourselves. We never got thanks and appreciation from the American people, but we gave it to ourselves, as long as we remember, those we left behind will never be forgotten.

We are finally able to lift our heads up and be proud of what we did as soldiers and as men. The political aspect of that war will be argued long after we are gone, but the courage and dedication we displayed can never be contested.

"The best to my brothers"

Jim Weander
U.S.M.C Vietnam Veteran
Vietnam Veterans Memorial Paddle-Out
September 30, 2007
Oceanside, California

TIME AND AGAIN

He told me what life was like as a young soldier in Vietnam. I told him what life was like as a young marine in Iraq. We are still fighting the same war, not much has changed. Same enemy, same guerrilla tactics, same military politics and the food still sucks!

The enemy back then, as now, was very evasive. One day they're talking to you as a friend offering you food and drinks in the village and the next day they put in roadside bombs and set up ambushes. We are constantly engaged by booby traps and the unknown.

"Same war, different country, one's desert, the other's jungle"

"Fuck them both"

Greg Murray
Scout/sniper, U.S.M.C., Fullajan, Iraq
Vietnam Veterans Memorial Paddle-Out
September 30, 2007
Oceanside, California

A HUMBLE WARRIOR

Few on Earth
have reached into their soul.
A man of combat
wears his soul on his chest everyday.
A soul exposed
is a heavy task for a mortal.
A soul usually
resides deep within.
The few, the proud
have mastered this.
Go ahead, speak of your Journey.
That's fine,
but take a day to walk in their shoes,
dare to even take a step,
or imagine what it would be
to try one on.

And become a Humble Warrior

CFC 333

IN LOVING MEMORY

Vietnam Veteran
PFC E3 Erving Joseph Martinez

1947-2010
Screaming Eagles 82nd Airborne Division
4 Purple Hearts
3 Bronze Stars
Silver Medal of Honor
Died of Agent Orange Related Cancer
God Rest His Soul, To A Place of Peace

IN LOVING MEMORY

Celebrating the Life of our Son
"Michael Matthew McGuirk aka "Magou"

September 8th, 1980 – October 8th, 2011

The Legacy he left behind, while he
watches from heaven.

Victoria and Michael McGuirk

www.straightupsolGier.com

SURFING SOLGIER

My husband and I drove to Daytona Beach 37 years ago, with our car painted "just married" and never left. A lot of people never knew that my son struggled with the "demons of being a victim of sexual abuse" and he never talked about it until recently. He was a very brave and courageous young man. When he was only nine years old, he faced his teacher who had sexually abused him and others for years. His testimony in 1990 sent this pedophile to prison for 170 years. He planned to start a foundation that would help sexually abused children.

He named his dream "Straight Up SolGier." The "G" is for God because he was a very spiritual person and he believed that you had to be strong to stand up to abuse and your abusers. He had a great respect for real soldiers having two cousins in active duty, with two uncles and Grandparents having been in the service. Matt created a beautiful and unique logo to represent his dream. If you look close you will see his face behind the logo, this was the face of the little boy that sat at the stand in 1990 facing his "demon" in the courtroom.

Matt found peace surfing the ocean and was constantly drawn to the water. In honor of Matt, his soul surfing buddies gathered together at Sunglow Pier in Daytona Beach for a paddle out ceremony on Sunday, October 16, 2011.

My son's ashes were in a specially designed shell that was made to dissolve in the ocean and was let go by his sister and my son's girlfriend who were in the middle of the circle. It was an amazing and very spiritual experience. It had been overcast all morning then suddenly during the ceremony there was a break in the clouds above. It was as though Matt was saying, "Hello and Thank you." You can see the sun glistening on the water in the picture. One lonely little dolphin lifted his head and leaped through the water, as if to again say "Hello" for Matt.

BLESSING 333

God Bless All
Who have given their lives
in unselfish Valor
For they are
the Chosen
Ones

CFC 333

www.ButterflyPeople.com

SPIRIT OF THE BUTTERFLY

In life we may be blessed with a visit from a messenger.

Such a visit took place on a trip my wife and I took to San Juan, Puerto Rico. A family tragedy in 2001 took the life of our son, Everett. Over the past years, we have connected his spirit in the form of a butterfly.

While walking the streets of Old San Juan, we were drawn into a shop with a magnificent environment of butterflies. It was a busy day, yet the owners found time to hear our story and console us with their wisdom of the spirit of the butterfly.

We left the shop with a feeling of peace and a connection to the universe.

Having walked two blocks on a crowded street, to our amazement the owner had left his busy shop and found us, handing my wife that special butterfly.

We thank Djat Revan and his lovely wife, Cirene, for their incredible kindness, for they are truly Messengers of the Universe.

BOOK REVIEWS

"*Camp Hero* is a beautifully written story about the pain of loss, the beauty of friendship and the priceless gift of life. This spiritually insightful and thought-provoking narrative allows us all to relate to the enormity of tragedy and the brotherhood of healing. It is a gift to all and a must read for injured souls seeking a path back from darkness."

—L. Bernardi

"This book came to me at a very difficult time in my personal life. I knew by the synopsis that it was a story of deep love, loss and relationships. I was unsure how I would receive it. As I moved forward deeper into the characters and story, I grew quickly attached. I was pleasantly surprised at how drawn I was to them, and how much I identified with their journeys. There was a healing that took place inside myself as I escaped into this piece of wonderful literature. Charles Carlino does a wonderful job as a storyteller. I look forward to more works by him. Long live the butterflies and bumble bees. I know you understand, Charles.....thank you."

—Sandy Harding

"This book mixes true stories with just the right amount of fiction to tell an unforgettable story that you will not want to put down. Sometimes things are created with a higher purpose and I believe *Camp Hero* is one of them."

—Marissa Danielle

"Amazing story that brings back to life the horror's of the experience of an American Marine during the Vietnam conflict in the 1960's and a gal from New Jersey who lost loved ones in the 9/11 tragedy. The author skillfully through his characters shows us the mental anguish that they suffered and how it affected their behavior moving forward. I was taken back by the way he takes us full circle to show us how two lives are intertwined spiritually to a fascinating conclusion and wonderment. The protagonist in *Camp Hero* is the author's lifelong friend and 'Hero.' This is a must read for "Boomers" and anyone who has been touched by a spiritual epiphany."

—Robert DiNapoli, M.D.

"I've read *Camp Hero* a number of times—sometimes in parts and segmented, as it was being written through the years—talking with the author for long periods of time of the story he wanted so strongly to convey. Now that I've had the honor of reading it in final form, I am blown away! This important story that claimed Carlino's heart and mind for many, many years is written beautifully, so thoughtfully, with such sincerity to help bring healing and hope to the broken souls who are honored in this story. *Camp Hero* can help to heal broken hearts, an intention that has been met with reality. It is incredibly written and poignantly portrayed through such vivid description and dialogue. This book will make a difference to many."

—Joyce Carlino

"*Camp Hero* is an authentic American story blending Long Island and California surf dreams with stories of life on the city streets of New York (circa 9/11) and tales of untold loss in the DMZ of Vietnam. It is vividly detailed and wonderfully told. Vignettes depicting the earthshaking personal consequences of 9/11 are interlaced with true accounts of U.S. veterans in country and home after Vietnam. This unlikely fusion builds to an unforgettable resolution and an undeniable revelation of the interconnectedness of all. Being the daughter of a veteran and a native New Yorker who started a new job in Manhattan only three weeks prior to 9/11, I felt a tangible healing effect in reading *Camp Hero*. I imagine many readers will share a kindred experience."

—Penolope Love

"An enlightening and very thought provoking, emotional read for me. The characters were very dear to my heart, having heard from friends the stories of the very sad and shameful way Americans greeted them back home after surviving Vietnam. Not only do they live with ghosts of war; they had to survive a slap in the face from fellow countrymen they sacrificed to serve and protect. I've also lived the fear of that waited call from loved ones working in the towers on 9-11. My family was one of the lucky ones who got a hug at the end of the day. We still mourn for the friends and coworkers that never made it home. Charles brought both story lines together with a very inspirational ending to both tragedies. Thank you, Charles, and a thank you to all veterans, active duty and first responders, for their courageous service and sacrifice to our great country."

—K C

"*Camp Hero* is an extraordinary drama that I was unable to put down. I was completely captivated by the drama that combines the horror's of the Vietnam War and the devastating events of 9/11. The author does an outstanding job to transcend the reader into the well-written storyline and ends with a fascinating conclusion. This book is a must read for everyone!"

—Robert Goldberg

"I was given this book by a friend and I took it on my vacation to Puerto Rico with the thought of reading it while on the beach. Needless to say, I read it in two days. I simply couldn't put it down. The story was well written, which made it easy to follow. It literally brought tears to my eyes by allowing me to experience the heartbreak of those affected by such a horrific tragedy. It also solidified my thoughts on how precious life is and how important it is to express love to those around you because tomorrow is never promised."

—Emily Mahan

"This message is needed more now than ever. It captures the common thread of painful, human tragedies and ultimately offers us hope. The beauty of this book is its attempt to provide glimpses of answers from a view of the Divine. The author challenges us to open our mind but more importantly, our souls."

—Jim Maun

ABOUT THE AUTHOR

Charles F. Carlino
Veteran United States Marine Corps
1967-1969

Marine Corps Training Station
Paris Island, SC

Charles F. Carlino was born in Brooklyn, New York, on December 20, 1947, to a middleclass Italian family. When he was six, his family moved to a small seaside town at the edge of Queens, where he grew up.

He attended Andrew Jackson High School, graduating class of June '65. Realizing a childhood dream, he was appointed lifeguard number '333' that summer. This number would become a significant connection of God's affirmation throughout his life. The next time these numbers showed up is when he joined the United States Marine Corp in 1967 during the Vietnam Crisis, his dog tags displaying:

"333"

His life placed closely to the Vietnam War and to the World Trade Disaster of 9/11 has given him an intimate perspective on the nature of the damage to their survivors—thus his story:

"Camp Hero"

A favorite movie, *Pay It Forward*, describes a sequence of events that connect action with reaction. The same sequence was experienced in his early childhood, after being saved by a stranger after falling through the ice. "Fate had me rescued that day in order that I may have the blessing to rescue others. My life has been filled with many brushes with death, only to receive God's pardon in order that I may save other lives.

"Most recently while surfing at Florida's Boynton Beach inlet during a storm, I spotted what looked like three heads bobbing on the surface a few hundred yards away to my right, near the mouth of the inlet. Surfing in the outer break with a strong southerly wash, I was not sure what to make of it and caught the next wave taking me to beach. Paddling back out to the outer break, I settled in.

Turning seaward, something told me to look for those bobbing heads and at that moment about fifty yards further out I spotted what looked to be a surfer on a short board. I called out but got no response. There were at least one hundred surfers in the immediate area and yet no one, not even the lifeguards on duty, were aware of this grave situation. Quickly paddling to the closest, now in the early throes of drowning and bleeding from being washed across the jetty, I pulled him onto my surfboard and yelled to another surfer who was at a distance to my right. Finally catching his attention, he and a small group of surfers headed out in the rough seas and rescued the remaining two. On that glorious day, God placed me in the roll to Pay it Forward and save the lives of these young men."

Mr. Carlino was a longstanding member of the Circle Repertory Theatre in New York City and now, a member of the Lake Worth Playhouse Advisory Board, Lake Worth, Florida.

OTHER WORKS BY CHARLES F. CARLINO

The Temple of the Sole Surfer

Moonlight Serenade, "The Passage"

If The Shoe Fits

Rainforest Monopoly

Expedia.Paradise

Master of Mediocrity

Weekend Warrior

The Cure

The Glass Bridge

TO MY READERS AND FRIENDS OF THE CAMP

If this book has brought to you
or someone you know
a sense of peace or spiritual healing,
please feel free to share a comment
or review in the online
Camp Hero
Book Reviews on Amazon.

And please join us on our
Camp Hero Memorial Blog
and send your message of healing
to the Universe:

www.CampHero-FriendsOnTheWall.com

Thank you